D0467514

NO ONE EVER
TOLD US THAT

Other Books by John D. Spooner

Fiction

*The Pheasant-Lined Vest of Charlie Freeman:
A Novel of Wall Street* (1967)

*Three Cheers for War in General:
A Novel of the Army Reserve* (1968)

Class (1973)

The King of Terrors (1975)

The Foursome (1993)

Nonfiction

Confessions of a Stockbroker (1972)

Smart People: A User's Guide to Experts (1979)

*Sex and Money: Behind the Scenes with the
Big-Time Brokers* (1985)

A Book for Boston (1980)

*Do You Want to Make Money or Would You
Rather Fool Around?* (1999)

NO ONE EVER TOLD US THAT

MONEY *and* LIFE LETTERS *to* My GRANDCHILDREN

JOHN D. SPOONER

BUSINESS
PLUS

NEW YORK   BOSTON

Business Plus
Hachette Book Group
237 Park Avenue
New York, NY 10017
www.HachetteBookGroup.com

Printed in the United States of America

RRD-C

First Edition: April 2012

Business Plus is an imprint of Grand Central Publishing.
The Business Plus name and logo are trademarks of Hachette Book Group, Inc.

The Hachette Speakers Bureau provides a wide range of authors for speaking events. To find out more, go to www.hachettespeakersbureau.com or call (866) 376-6591.

The publisher is not responsible for websites (or their content) that are not owned by the publisher.

10 9 8 7 6 5 4 3 2 1

Library of Congress Cataloging-in-Publication Data
Spooner, John D.
  No one ever told us that : money and life letters to my grandchildren / John D. Spooner.—1st ed.
    p. cm.
  Includes bibliographical references.
  ISBN 978-1-4555-1155-6
  1. Investments—Miscellanea.   2. Finance, Personal—Miscellanea.
3. Conduct of life—Miscellanea.   I. Title.
  HG4521.S7183 2012
  650.1—dc23   2011044775

For my grandchildren:
Alyssa, Wesley, Marlo, Teague, and Gala.
And above all, for Mimi,
the founder of the feast.

Acknowledgments

Grandchildren:

All life is relationships. On that score, several extraordinary people who truly get it offered me wisdom and encouragement through the writing of this book. In no special order they are: Peggy Hogan and Steve Hill, Louie Howland, Bill Phillips, Bill Whitworth, Scott Abell, Peter Flaherty, Dwight Crane, David Tobias, Joe O'Donnell, Lay Lee Ong, and my editorial right arm, Yvonne Russell.

And as I've told you, Alyssa and Wesley, one of the keys to business success is closing the deal. Here's a special toast to my agent, John Taylor "Ike" Williams, and my editor, Rick Wolff.

Author's Note

I see dozens of young people every year, most of them eager to have careers in finance or in journalism. But in the last several years, I'm increasingly seeing college graduates having problems getting any job or finding new ones after being let go from where they started. All of these graduates have been eager for personal stories about being in the business trenches over the last fifty years. They particularly liked tales of problems, bumps in the road, bear markets, political missteps, and how people reacted to the tough stuff. So this book is not just for my grandchildren about to emerge into a challenging adult world. It's for all of you children and grandchildren, with too few practical mentors, who can all use some advice from someone with lots of bruises, someone still standing and still up for the game.

John D. Spooner
Winter 2011

Contents

NO ONE EVER
TOLD US THAT

Introduction

I know it's old-fashioned, but I love letters. I love to write them and receive them. I enjoy the quality of the stationery and the hardness of fine card stock. And, as in many things in life, I enjoy the anticipation; what's in the note or letter? And I think more weight is given to something handwritten. Often, the real letters are saved as a memory of something special.

When I was sent out to summer camp at age nine, I was ordered by my father to write home. "Not just 'I played baseball' or 'went swimming'; 'send comic books,'" he said. "I want letters of *substance*: what you're seeing, what you're feeling, what your new friends are like." My father was tough and demanded recognition that what I received was never to be taken for granted.

This discipline continued when I went to college, when I first visited Europe, when I was in the Army

Medical Corps stationed in San Antonio. Often it was a real pain in the neck to write, another chore like taking out the trash or shoveling the snow off the driveway. My father never wrote to me. It was a one-way street because, with him, I was continually being tested. He made his philosophical points verbally, peppering me from childhood on with his observations on life. Here are a few: "Life is work, whether you want to hear it or not." And "Life is hard, punctuated by moments of brilliance," "Marry funny," "The paths of glory lead but to the grave" (from the poem "Elegy Written in a Country Churchyard" by Gray), "If you only read three books in your life, read *War and Peace*, Gibbon's *Decline and Fall of the Roman Empire*, and James T. Farrell's *Studs Lonigan*."

In my freshman year in college my father gave me a copy of *Studs Lonigan*, which tracks the childhood and young manhood of a kid from the mean streets of Chicago in the 1930s. It was a raw slice of life, profane, and in the view of many critics obscene. I liked it a lot and gave my copy to my girlfriend at the time. When her father found out she was reading it and that I had given it to her, I was banned from his house. He actually said, "That boy will never darken my door again." I really like old-fashioned. But the father and daughter flunked the "marry funny" principle. And that was the end of that.

My mother wrote me letters when I went to camp, to college, and to the army. She was prepared for the task because she had kept a daily diary from age ten to practically until she married my father. In the 1920s, as a teenager, chronicling her adolescent years, every four or five pages she would say, "Fell off the roof today. What a bore." And again, "Fell off the roof. Headache and tummy ache will *not* stop me from going to the Tea Dance at the Copley." "Falling off the roof" was shorthand for having her period. She wrote me opinionated, personal, bitchy observations, sprinkled with warnings as well: "Don't follow the crowd wherever they go, they always wear the worst clothes, like brittle corduroys. Avoid anyone who, when they walk, the noise is 'swish, swish.'"

This all reinforces my love for letters. I wrote notes to my children, often accompanied by checks, which seemed to carry more force than the notes, full of platitudes: "Go get 'em," "Study hard," "Don't mix Scotch and vodka." I'm lucky. I have grandchildren. And I now have the time, with them in their college years, to write them proper letters on all sorts of subjects. About money, or the lack of it. And business. I am writing to them the lessons that only come from the tough stuff in life, the absurd, the bumps, the heroes and heroines.

There is a line about grandparents and grandchildren and why they tend to get along so well: "Because they

have a common enemy." So I'm writing to my grandchildren, who are on the cusp of becoming something
scary: grown-ups. I hope I'll tell them about things no
one else has brought to their attention, like the emotional content of stock markets; about cycles of fear and
greed; about how to separate the phony from the real;
about the wisdom of not being a headline reader and
the necessity of forming long-term plans.

These letters will be grumpy, contrary, sometimes
rambling, colorful, and sardonic. They will also be full
of tales of the lure and dangers and intrigue of money.
And they will be loving as well.

John D. Spooner

Getting Jobs

Dear Alyssa and Wesley:

This will be the first of, I hope, many letters to you in college. But I have to tell you up front that you don't have to save them. I won't be hurt or offended if you throw them out, but I'll also tell you that, years from now, you'll be sorry you tossed them in the trash. There is a somewhat dispassionate and bemused feeling that grandparents have about grandchildren. We do not have to raise you the way we did our own kids. We have no axe to grind. Therefore, in my opinion, grandparents can give advice that often parents are afraid of giving, for fear you may interpret it the wrong way.

This grandfather has no fear. I have worked for fifty years and kept my eyes and ears wide open. But you should understand early on that I believe in the absurdity of life and have been looking for practical solutions to problems in business and with money and personal relationships all that time. I hope to pass on these observations to make your lives both richer and even amusing. Amusing means a lot. And you can take that to the bank. Just make sure you take it to a bank that is solvent.

Today's ramble is about getting jobs, once you are out in life. It's the first of many things I'll share with you that I've had to learn the hard way.

Several years ago I spoke to a group of international graduate students at Brandeis University. They were all anxious about what was next in their lives, and I talked with them about searching for jobs. I told them that I see dozens of young people each year who want to come into the financial world and are desperate for words to put them on the right path. First thing I tell them is "Never call a busy person first thing on Monday morning." Busy people are getting into their business routines for the week and the last person they want to hear from when they begin that week is you, because you represent a freebie, someone who is nonproductive for them, wasting their time no matter how worthy you are. And you, all eager to get on with life, are just going to annoy them if you call first thing Monday morning. Call Tuesday afternoon, after lunch.

By then busy people are more accepting of these calls because they are into the rhythm of the week and over the often-unsettling fact of Monday mornings. My friend Peter Solomon, former chairman of now defunct Lehman Brothers, told me, after I mentioned this advice, "You know, when I was in the midst of any big deal, I would never call any of the key players until Tuesday. If I called them Monday morning, they would think something was wrong."

You think your "Papa" only pays attention to you. But I also see hundreds of résumés a year, from people of all ages wanting jobs, wanting advice about jobs. Almost all of the résumés are pretty plain vanilla: education, work history. Boring. And the vast percentage of résumés sent out blind automatically get tossed into the circular file— the wastebasket. What *will* get you the job is something you may think trivial but that jumps out at the person scanning the résumé, something that possibly has nothing to do with educational record or job history. "Is there anything special about you?" I ask them. "Any sports history in school? Any hobby out of the ordinary, anything you collect or in which you have an unusual interest?"

"Well," a recent young interviewee said to me, "I rowed crew in college, on a championship team, but it was the past. I didn't think it was relevant."

"Don't you know that there are clubs in life?" I said to her. "Secret places in the heart that others around the world will respond to instantly? Why? Because those others were members of those secret clubs as well." Crew is one of these clubs. So are rugby and lacrosse and sailing and wrestling. So are field hockey and swim team and women's ice hockey and basketball and school radio stations and Gilbert and Sullivan performances. And amateur rock or heavy metal bands. *Put these kinds of things on your résumés, personal things that jump out at the reader.* The unexpected passions from the past are what will get you jobs much more readily than academic achievement. Never lie about these hobbies or interests, but trumpet them vigorously. Aside from getting you jobs, they have made your lives inevitably more interesting and will continue to do so. You may say, "Give us an example." So I will.

A young man based in Japan for several years called me, desperately wanting to relocate with his young family back to the United States. But his fluency in Japanese, he told me, put him in a box where people needed him more over there than in America. His résumé looked fine, but had absolutely no life to it; a grey corporate past. I asked him if he pursued any hobbies. There were none listed on his CV. "I'm a black belt in karate," he responded. I got him to add this to his résumé. Within weeks he had a strong response and several job offers to relocate to New York and Boston. The offers came from CEOs who, during interviews with him, spent the bulk of the sessions asking about the dedication and discipline it took to become a black belt. *The unusual aspects of your life can not only enhance and enrich your experience, they can open doors and keep them open.*

One of the kids in the audience at Brandeis raised his hand and said, "Thank you. No one ever told us that."

In your case, Wesley, you worked on a cod fishing boat in high school; mention that in your résumé. And your strong interest in old coins, and yes, lacrosse. Sounds odd, but it will intrigue others.

Alyssa, your early interest in teaching young people, as if you had a calling for it—I've always thought that was so appealing. This sensitivity and caring for others is something that smart interviewers will warm to.

My letters to you, I hope, will not be long on clichés. I want to keep you wide awake, not nodding off.

Your loving and ever-curious Papa

The unusual aspects of your lives can open doors.

The Importance of the Past

Grandchildren:

I'm going to be jumping around a lot, just to let you know—no theme, no overall plot. Why? Because life is random, accidental in so many ways.

Someone told me years ago that the best compliment you could pay to anyone was "You're never boring." Even though I couldn't verbalize this as a kid, my grandfather (your great-great-grandfather) was an early model for me in this regard. I've told you some stories about him, but never anything about his business and money advice. Here's some of that.

Your great-great-grandfather was a tough little guy, about five feet five, but with broad shoulders, a big chest, and big hands like a baseball catcher, which he was in his youth. You've seen two pictures of him in my study.

One is with his semiprofessional ball team, the Hemlocks, in 1907 on Boston Common.

The other photo from a few years later is of him in an amateur opera production of *Pagliacci,* dressed in a clown costume, the tenor and star. This was in the North End of Boston, then and now the Italian section of Boston. He could not speak English when he came to America. His parents and their four children lived in a North End tenement apartment with two bedrooms and one bathtub. The tub they filled with coal to use for their winter heat. Your great-great-grandfather's goal was to become American as quickly as possible. The same was true for his friends. Partly this was so important because he remembered soldiers of the Russian czar, the Cossacks, riding through his village in Poland, killing, looting, sticking bayonets into straw in the barns, hoping people were hiding there.

In Boston, he boxed professionally in his late teens under the name "Kid Manning" because, he told me, "No one was ever going to attack me or my family without me defending them." For a long time he thought men with bayonets would storm into their apartment in Boston. He had dreams about it. Why tell you about all this? Because I want you two to realize that I didn't make any of this up. These stories are in your blood. And so you will understand early that the most incredible things in life are not plucked from novels. They're *true.*

Another reason for stories from the past, particularly stories of hardship overcome, is the climate you're going to find when you both graduate. I have never seen, in all the bumps in my life, a climate in American society like the one we entered into about three years ago when stock markets and the economy began to melt down. Your generation will be facing tougher sledding than any generation has since the 1930s. Many people are either ignorant of the changes around us or lost in denial. But I'll talk a lot about what I think you can expect when you're both launched into this new order, after school. Don't despair, however. For curious, imaginative people, there will be great opportunities.

This week's note is a quickie, a teaser if you will. Not an excuse for brevity, but your Papa, believe it or not, has a busy week ahead, beyond writing to you.

Yours in haste,
Papa

Stay in touch with your past.

What I Learned from the Military

Wesley and Alyssa:

Believe it or not, before Vietnam began, in the late 1950s and early 1960s, there was a military draft on in America. This meant that if you were a young man, you *had* to serve in the armed forces, unless you were either physically unfit (such as having a heart murmur) or psychologically unfit (subject to interpretation).

Most of my friends and I opted to enlist in the Reserves—Army, Air Force, or Marine Corps. This meant for me serving for six months of active duty in the army, followed by five and a half years of Reserve training, one night a week, one weekend a month, and two weeks at different bases in the summer. If I had it to do over, I would have just served full time for two years and gotten it finished. I enjoyed the entire first six months and hated the Reserve training later. Active duty was an education. The Reserves were for the "weekend war-riors" and almost, in my view, a complete waste of time.

In my summer training, I was made unit historian. This, I quickly learned, allowed me to wander at will with a clipboard, taking notes. It also allowed me to leave Camp Drum, in upstate New York, in uniform. Off base I could head to a nearby lake and work on a novel for two or three hours. The novel was about the Army Reserve (*Three Cheers for War in General*, the title an ironic quote from Mussolini). It was really M*A*S*II dur-ing peacetime.

Two silly but useful things I learned from my army experience that you can transfer into life outside the military:

1. Always look as though you know exactly where you're going, even if you don't. Walk purposefully, focused on the horizon, and no one will ever stop you to order you on to work details. This will be true on all of your jobs.
2. It helps a lot if you carry a clipboard. People will think you're official. This will work in your job as well. Carrying a tablet won't help you; the boss will think you're surfing the Net or exploring things non-job-related. A clipboard means business to others.

The cosmic lessons were many. Basic infantry training invariably collected men from everywhere in America. They were rich, dirt poor, and in between, every
color of the rainbow. We lived cheek by jowl, in stacked
bunk beds. Reveille: "You gotta get up, you gotta get up,
you gotta get up this morning," went the old Irving Berlin song. And we did. At 5:30 a.m., lined up on the company street, half asleep, knowing we had to shape up.
Because if we didn't, everyone in the unit would suffer.

So we pulled together, Puerto Ricans from San
Juan, who slept with their bayonets under their pillows,
because they were told the gringos would attack them in
their sleep. We had an East Boston contingent, all Italian,
wising off on the bus to Fort Dix, joking together, the
coolest of cool. Later many of them cried and fainted in
the shot line. They had never had inoculations. This was
amazing to me, the young innocent from the suburbs.
Amazing that these East Boston guys, street smart, so
on top of it going to basic training, could have fears and
anxieties just like me.

But we all learned to adapt, to trust and learn from
one another. I also discovered that there was a class of
people I never knew existed, a special cadre of people called "sergeants." I learned that the sergeants ran
the army and, more than any other rank, commanded
respect from the troops. They commanded fear, too,

because we wanted to please them. And they commanded love as well.

I also learned that human beings are incredibly resilient and can adapt to almost any condition. Grandchildren, it's good to be tested. And the testing—someone viewing us, passing judgment—will never stop. You will build up scar tissue from the bumps life gives you, and the tough testing helps.

This letter, I think, wants to begin talking to you about service, and I suppose it's advice you can pass on to younger friends who have to deal with the increasing burden of student loans. College costs are obscene, way out of proportion to inflation and, in my opinion, way out of proportion to what so many colleges offer to you. Definitely not value added.

Service to your country, in many areas, carries scholarship and credit benefits in exchange for your time and effort.

This service is not just military. It can be the Peace Corps; it can be City Year in Boston. I just heard from one of my business partners that her niece, in dental school, will get credit toward her tuition for work on an Indian reservation.

Service can help pay for education. Service can get you out into the world without crushing debt that you have to pay off for years.

But it can also send you into full-time employment

with an appreciation for people up and down the scales of society. If you have a better sense of our diverse population it will make you appreciate the bounties you both have been blessed with. And this understanding will make you both much smarter.

Your Papa, who learns the darndest
things from all kinds of people

Never close your minds.

Dare to Be Different

Wesley and Alyssa:

One of the sad aspects of modern life is the pitifully short attention span of most young people: too many distractions, too much competition for the ears and eyes. Most of my letters to you will be fairly brief, although I would never place either of you in the "most young people" category. You both, of course, are superior in every way. At least until I ask your parents about you. Technology is second nature to you both, but will always be somewhat a mystery to me. But revolutions come and go. The buzzwords and the characters change in history, creativity and revolutions happen: the Industrial Revolution, the automobile, radio, television, the Internet.

But remember this as a number-one key to understanding business and life: *Human nature never changes.*

Think about kids from your childhoods who were little princesses, nerds, jocks, snobs, bullies. Try to imagine them as adults, or maybe you know what happened to them. Focusing on those childhood people will make you shake your head and realize that not much changes in character from playground days. This can help you a lot in business, if you ask fellow workers about their childhoods. Stories will come flooding out that can help you evaluate *your* futures.

Human nature never changes. This thought almost totally governs stock market behavior, and it comes to me with the perspective of watching markets and people's behavior for over fifty years. I have had a handful of clients during that time who have always, because of emotions, made exactly the wrong moves, time and time again.

These people sold after every true panic I have seen: after President John F. Kennedy's assassination; after the huge market crash of 1987; after the 9/11 attacks. After every panic, markets eventually moved to all-time highs. They bought in the electronics boom at the end of the 1960s, bought tax shelters in the 1980s, bought Internet stocks at the top in 2001. The greed bubbles destroyed stock valuations in those sectors.

If, and for some people it's a big if, you believe in the future of America, then believe that when headlines scream, "Fear!" you should be looking to nibble at real estate, stocks, paintings, and collectibles. When you feel it in your gut that you should be very afraid, the world around you will scream, "Nothing will ever be good again." Dare to go against the grain; dare to buy a first apartment or house; buy a drawing by a young artist you admire; buy a stock to believe in for the long haul. Be a contrarian.

You both are lucky in many ways, including that you both have been to France. I first visited there when I graduated from college and traveled with two friends with whom I had acted in school musicals. We sang for meals and lodging and drinks, never paying more than two dollars apiece for a room, in the days when the American dollar was king and queen. (Excuse the ramblings, but our family has always loved stories. Sometimes I even ask your grandmother when we shut the lights, "Tell me a story." Sometimes she does. Childish, right? You should *always* keep hints of childhood in your life, I think.)

Back to France. Other than the kings and queens whom you've studied (I hope), probably the wealthiest family, perhaps for several hundred years, has been the Rothschilds. One of the early counts of the family, when asked by a young man for the secret to making money on the Bourse (the French stock market), supposedly said, "When the streets of Paris are running with blood, I buy." Be a contrarian. Bet against the crowd. You will thrive when others look back and grind their teeth. Never be afraid to be different.

Your different (if diffident) Papa

Human nature never changes.

Good Accidents in Life

Alyssa and Wes:

Greetings to the college kids. I often wish I were back there as well.

This letter is about accidents in life. I have a client who chairs a foundation in New York. It's an almost $700 million foundation. I mention the number because I think big numbers are amorphous. What do they mean? There are more than a billion people in China, more than 300 million in the United States. These numbers are so large as to render them squishy. I actually don't like or trust numbers too much. I was so bad in math, I was allowed to skip second-year algebra in high school and take art instead. When I went into the world of finance my friends laughed. I did get a D in first-year algebra and a C in geometry, so I had serious doubts myself. All I wanted to do was write.

But, as you know, my dad was a partner in an old investment firm. We were good little boys and girls in the days just before Vietnam heated up. We feared going to the headmaster's office and, if you can believe it, we *really* feared our fathers. Back then, fathers as a class did not care to be our best buddies or live to glorify their children. They lived to rule their households. Mostly with an iron hand. My father would actually say to me when I was little and had misbehaved, "Get me my strap." Not only was I going to get spanked, I had to *fetch* the damn instrument. I now think it's funny, and I never had to get "help" with the concept in later years. But as *your* father probably told you, I never hit my own children. Psychological warfare was enough (only kidding).

My father announced to me when I graduated from college, "You're coming into the investment business." "But, Dad," I said, "I can't even read the stock page in the newspaper. I have zero interest in the market. I want to be a writer." He threw me a challenge. "You're coming into this business. But if you want to write badly enough, you'll find the time." I was determined to find the time. I was determined to write my way to freedom, and *when*—not *if*—my first book was published, I'd be out the door. Remember this lesson I will repeat as the "accidental nature of life." By the time I finished my first novel and sold it to a publisher, it took three years. And during that time, I made an incredible discovery:

the stock market was all about human nature, not math. Fear and greed. The only thing I thought I knew about in those days was character. I had, totally by accident, found the perfect business for me. So have an open mind for the possibility of accidents happening.

As a bonus in this letter, I will try to ask a question you will probably raise with each other: "What about family businesses? Good idea or bad?" In watching people's money over all these years, I'll tell you that family can be a killer. When I was under my dad's thumb early in my career, it was bad—me as the idiot child. As time went on, Dad got older, I gained more confidence, and I was becoming the father. This was worse than the early days. My advice is to go make your own path in life, avoid the baggage, the politics, the infighting of family affairs. And if you come back in triumph, family will still be a killer. You deserve honesty from me.

Your loving grandfather

Know your characters.

There Are Many Ways to the Truth

Grandchildren:

My father gave me some bad advice while I was growing up, and he gave me some good advice as well. The bad advice had to do with foolish myths. Like when he told me, "Before you marry, look at the mother of the woman you presumably love. If you cannot stand her mother, think long and hard about the daughter. Most women eventually turn into their mother."

The good advice that I took to heart included "Never expect anyone else to do anything for you. Expect to do it yourself." Remembering this lesson, I have never dwelled on being disappointed with what others didn't do for me. It will be important for both of you to do this as well, not as a cynical response to events in your life, but as a realistic (if sad) reaction to the way things work. When and if you do get unexpected boosts in life from others, put it in the category of nice surprises and still be prepared to fend for yourselves.

On with this week's lesson in self-reliance. How are you going to build up your own net worth? Here's key advice from someone I was thrown in with by accident, someone whose early words to me gave me the base so that if I never go into an office again, your grandmother (your Mimi) and I can live the good life for the rest of our years.

My first investment firm went broke in the early 1970s. Literally hundreds of well-known companies closed down because they could not handle the volume of business that was building; they could not handle 20-million-share days, in this time before computers. Today, daily volume on the New York Stock Exchange often trades more than a *billion* shares. If you ordered 100 shares of IBM in the 1970s, you might be delivered a certificate for 1,000 shares of Ford Motor. If you expected a check for $600, you might get one for $6,000. Chaos. No controls. My company went bankrupt and merged with a new firm founded by four young Wall Street upstarts, rookies really, with little experience but with brains and guts.

One of the four partners was a college classmate of mine. He took me to lunch in Boston, trying to convince me not to defect to a competing firm. I listened and made the comment to him that the stock market was so low he could probably buy shares in the many companies that looked cheap to me. He had a wolflike smile and turned it on. "I'm actually leaving the firm myself," he said. "Why buy cheap stocks when you can go out and buy the companies themselves?" That was my first lesson in looking at changing conditions in business in different ways. The conventional boring way was to buy cheap stocks. The creative, entrepreneurial approach was to go out and try to buy the companies themselves. There are many ways to the truth.

The next letter will get back to getting half-baked rich in the stock market, the concept I hinted at earlier. I don't want to test your attention span. And I do get carried away. Not a good habit.

Your loquacious Papa

P.S. I know, I know—you know vocabulary. But it's actually good if you ever have to look up (or search) for the meaning of new words.

One size doesn't fit all.

It's the Emotions

Wesley and Alyssa:

This might be the most important lesson I could give you about investing. There have been thousands of books on this subject. But very few concentrate on what I think is the single biggest lesson to learn when investing your money in anything, but particularly in common stocks, because they are the most liquid of anything you hope to buy and sell for profit. Liquid means they are easy to buy and sell. In today, out tomorrow, if you wish.

Most of the thousands of books on the subject have been written by onlookers. Or economists. Or by ghostwriters for business CEOs. Almost none have been written by people who actually walk the walk, who invest their own and other people's money. I've been doing it for more than fifty years, for thousands of people, old and young, men and women, Americans and foreigners as well.

My first office manager, a great student of human nature, used to tell me that "the investment game is an Alice in Wonderland business. The money is real. But, because you can see the prices of your holdings day by day, minute by minute, people will be influenced *always* by the emotions of those minutes, particularly by fear and greed." This is probably the single best lesson I've ever received in the investment world. Followed closely by "If you want to truly get rich...concentrate, don't diversify."

Here's a little story about the fear side of the equation. Nine-eleven was a horrific day in American history. It shocked America to its core. My office staff, in my building before I arrived, would not let me come up in the elevator from the lobby, because they were sure our office would be attacked. Several people were hysterical. Then our building was closed and we all went home. That night a client called, a man who was sure the end of the world was upon us. "Sell everything," he yelled into the phone.

I pointed out to him that the markets were closed until the threat to America was somewhat understood and addressed. Markets closed precisely because no one in charge wanted panic selling to overwhelm them. This had happened in the past in dangerous times, like after President Kennedy's assassination. Often the best advice during tragedies like these is to take a step back and coolly consider the options.

"Never mind closed," yelled my client. "What do I pay you for? You can find a way. Get me *out*." Hysterical seldom does anyone any good.

I tried to calm him down, to no avail. When markets did reopen, prices plunged, but not in my view as much as they would have if the market had been allowed to stay open through the chaos. And if my client had stayed the course and sold nothing, which he did not, his portfolio in a few months would have been worth more than it was before the attacks.

Here's my take on the panics I've seen and lived through.

You should have—in *every* case—been a buyer of stocks, not a seller. And this is after watching people's money, as I have said, for such a long time.

I've never written to you about this, but I have always had about five "key" clients. No, not the big ones, the multimillion-dollar households. My five key clients, and they have changed over the years, are foolproof indicators of market behavior. They have *always* initially gone in the wrong direction. Some people are great at instant decisions. Most people are terrible at it. I'm bad at it myself, always have needed time to step back, consider the pros and cons, ponder what seems to be real and what isn't. And then I act.

By the way, these five bellwether clients who are *always* wrong are always also highly educated, most with graduate degrees. Why have they been so unsuc-cessful as investors? Because they have been taught that the universe is rational. The stock market, at its extremes, is never rational. It's an Alice in Wonderland business.

Greed, of course, is the flip side of fear, always close to the surface, wanting to break out. The last really greedy period in the stock market was at the end of the twentieth century, going into 2001 and 2002. There was a frenzy for Internet stocks, almost *any* Internet stock. "John doesn't understand the new exciting society," clients would say to my staff, never to me. "My neighbor's getting rich." Finally it got to be too much for one of my clients, a man who had been with me for years.

"I can't stand it," he said. "This may be my last chance to cash in."

"Don't tell me," I answered. "Your neighbor's getting rich."

"Worse!" he yelled. "Much worse. My brother-in-law's getting rich!"

Hundreds of newly public Internet stocks went to zero when the bubble broke in 2002. My client's brother-in-law had a stroke and died. Greed. Almost none of the people I knew who bought into the Internet bubble came out with anything but pennies on the dollar. Greed. And the frenzy to get rich quick.

I've said this before: Fads in almost every area—fashion, furnishings, stocks particularly—run for about two years. Then, look out below. Every time you feel greedy or fearful, stop and think, "Should I really be doing the opposite of what my emotions tell me?"

Just your Papa, planting the seeds

Fear and greed rule the markets.

Getting Rich in the Stock Market: Concentration

Good day, good Grandchildren:

Back to basics here, continuing on my early lessons on how to hit a home run in the stock market. (Even though it does take more than nine innings. Indeed, it takes more than several *seasons.*) But here it is, and it involves a concept I'll be talking to you about probably forever: the accidental nature of life. It was an accident that my original firm went broke. It was an accident that we were brought out of bankruptcy by a company eventually headed by the man who changed my financial life, Sandy Weill.

Sandy was a tough-minded young man from Brooklyn who had gone to Cornell. He talked himself into a job initially, as many doors on Wall Street were closed in those days to a brash Jewish kid from Brooklyn. Brooklyn kids, I've found, don't take "no" gently, have long memories, and will work their tails off to make their visions come true. Sandy and his partners began gobbling up Wall Street firms that were failing and throughout the 1970s built their firm into a powerhouse retail and institutional brokerage force.

After six months at my new job, I went to New York to see clients and got in to talk to our chairman, Sandy Weill. He was smoking a large cigar and staring at a quote machine, no TV or news, just New York Stock Exchange prices rolling by. He never looked up at me. "I'm in the middle of a few trades," he said, "staying on top of it. I hear I should read your last book, but I appreciate the business you're doing for us probably more than I'd appreciate the book." Sandy grilled me about Boston, what I thought of the firm, my opinion of its people, and what stocks I liked.

In those days, everyone in the business was a stock junkie: the market is an addictive business. And I know dozens of people who chose the business over their families. They got divorced. The adrenaline rush in anything can be fabulous, but also dangerous. Getting carried away on the highs can cost you a lot, both emotionally and personally.

In my entire conversation with Sandy Weill, he never looked at me, just at the numbers. And yet in a weird way, it didn't bother me. He felt the same way I did; never fitting the mold, on the outside looking in, creating his own reality. If you didn't like it, take a hike. Suddenly he said, "I want all of my employees to get rich, and to start to think like owners, not worker bees." "Sounds good to me," I said. At the time, I had lost all of my money in my old firm. I was thirty-six years old, with a mortgage and three little kids. And we were in a horrible bear market, one of the worst since the 1930s.

"You *can* get rich," Sandy went on, "even if you don't own the business—if you own enough stock and the stock goes up over many years." He whipped around in his chair and stared directly at me. I pulled back, surprised at his intensity. "*If*," he went on, "you *concentrate* and don't diversify. You want to get rich, work to understand the business and *lean on it*. Put it on black." That term is from roulette in a casino, betting on black or red numbers.

What he meant, and the advice I've followed since then, is what I call my "stake in life" stock theory. At your age, *growth* should be your goal: make your money and savings grow. My stake in life theory involves picking a public company you really believe in for the future and buying a few shares. How do you pick the company? Think Apple, years ago, or Amazon. Or pick a theme, like energy, or health care, or entertainment. Or pick a country that you think will thrive for years in a global economy, like China or India. If I were picking today, with twenty-twenty hindsight, I'd probably say that Exxon (energy) and Caterpillar Tractor (equipment for farming and building projects all over the world) would have been incredible investments for the last thirty or forty years. Buy a few shares and, preferably in weak stock markets, buy a few more shares. Keep buying, perhaps over years, reinvesting dividends (which you can do automatically) in more stock.

My biggest stake in life stock is American Express (cost me $6, now $48, and was $65 before the recent economic crunch). This investment in American Express has also spun off to me two of their subsidiaries over the years that were also home runs: Lehman Brothers, which I donated to charity long before it went broke, and Ameriprise, a financial services company that appreciated wonderfully.

Let's talk about this concept some more, as in, how do we pick a long-term investment and also, how long is long, in the time department? I wish someone had written to me about all of this. But the letters I got from home were all about "Use the extra blanket; take your medicine; don't get a chill; wear your galoshes." Geez.

Love to you both,
Papa

Own a lot of what you know and understand.

Getting In and Out of Debt

Grandchildren:

Time to talk a little about debt. Sometimes, "debt" is not such a dirty word; sometimes debt is outright evil. My father never forgot the 1930s, the Great Depression. He was an orphan at eleven and bounced from relative to relative. He worked on Wall Street during the late 1920s and early 1930s and was wiped out in the market crash at the time because he traded on margin. Margin equals debt—borrowing on the stocks you buy.

Quick example: You buy 100 shares of a stock at 50. It would cost you $5,000. On margin, say you put up 50 percent of the purchase price, or $2,500. The rest you borrow from the brokerage firm and pay them interest on the $2,500 you borrow. Say the interest is 10 percent. That's $250 a year you pay the broker. If the stock plunges, the broker can call you and ask for more money (collateral) to support your position in that stock. If you don't have the extra money, they can sell it out from under you. And you can lose *all* of your original $2,500. That, in a nutshell, is what happened massively in the 1930s. And individually to my dad.

It colored his entire adult life and he constantly hammered at me to *save*. And to eliminate all debt, wherever possible. "Debt is a killer," he would say. Today I owe *nothing* to anyone. No mortgages. No margin account debt. Only current monthly bills, like to phone companies or cable. This is boring but important, for debt is a cosmic or "big picture" lesson.

What about other forms of debt, like credit cards? I got my first card when I was in basic training in the Army Medical Corps. (I actually know how to take out your appendix.) It was an American Express card and I felt like a big deal because I thought, Gee, I must be a success, I've got my own AMEX card.

In those days, you had to pay off your card charges completely within thirty days of getting your bill. No partial payments—all of it. After several weeks in army basic training I was summoned to headquarters. "You've got an urgent long distance call, Spooner," they told me. Being an optimist, I actually thought, It's my literary agent, she's going to tell me that she's sold my first book to a publisher. I picked up the phone on the sergeant's desk, and a strange voice said, "John Spooner?"

"That's me," I answered.

"This is American Express calling. About your over-due bill. You run the risk of interest charges on the unpaid balance and losing your card." I still remember this shock of someone coming after me for money. It scared me.

Contrast this with today. I questioned an intern in our office and asked about credit cards.

"We're not AMEX people," she said. "We can't pay off our cards each month. We couldn't live if we couldn't pay these off bit by bit." Debt is a killer. I had to bail out my sister, paying off her MasterCard debt some years ago. And I paid off the debt of one of my assistants who got in big trouble with plastic more recently.

One of the big changes I see coming in society is your generation in general not having the free and easy life you've enjoyed so far. I know, you'll look at each other and roll your eyes. But I'm not senile yet. And I realize that every generation thinks the younger genera-tion is going to hell. I don't think *that*. But I know that you and your friends are going to have it much tougher. It *is* convenient to have credit cards. And it does give you flexibility, particularly when and if you travel. And, since life is mostly not pure—it is fuzzy—you'll need flexibility. If you cannot pay off a credit card in full every month, at least set yourself a debt limit that is realistic in terms of your earnings. For instance, agree with yourself that one thousand dollars is the most you'll allow yourself to borrow. It's your safety valve, if you will. Stick with it.

A further note here: I've recently done a survey of a dozen young people in their twenties and thirties. They all carry debit cards and all swear by them. "Let the debit card have the limits," they agree. "Say your parents put in a thousand dollars in your checking account. You use your card but you cannot exceed the amount in the account. It will be refused. This is the emergency fund, for a flat tire all alone in the wee hours, for instance." I'm persuaded by this. Common sense is common sense, wherever we hear it.

When your grandmother and I were first married, her sister Barbara lived in London. We wanted to visit for the fun and games, but no cash in our checking account. No savings either. I convinced a banker downstairs from my office to give me a three-thousand-dollar line of credit. We paid no interest until we actually wrote a check on the credit line. It was frivolous, but we spent two thousand dollars on the trip to London and a weekend in Paris. It was a romantic adventure and, early in our marriage, a great thing to do. (It can be great late in a marriage as well.) Long ago I paid off what I owed. That was forty years ago and I still see the original three-thousand-dollar credit available to me on my checking account for a rainy day. Whew! This last story illustrates the judicious use of debt to enhance our lives in small ways.

Your faithful correspondent
and your Papa (trying to enhance *your* lives)

Debt can be a killer.

Rules for If You Marry

Grandchildren:

Here's a surprise for young people. There's a full moon tonight, and full moons always make me think about romance. I was first really conscious of romance when I was working as a junior counselor in Maine, desperate for a girlfriend. Among the more than 300 million people in America, loneliness is a major problem. And loneliness can extend to every age, young or old. I bring this up because this subject is high on the list of anyone your age, particularly high (I'll bet) because you share my romantic gene. And you are majoring in chemistry, Wesley, and marine biology, Alyssa; two majors not loaded with romance or the dangers as well as pleasures in its pursuit. But romance will arrive when you least expect it.

My father, whom you never knew, was a really tough guy, as I've told you. When I was a freshman in college and dating someone my parents disliked (because of her parents), my father told me, "There are at least a thousand kinds of love and a thousand women from here to California who you could fall for and marry. There's no such thing as one person for one person." Cynical, right? But your great-grandpa was a history buff and entitled to his opinion.

These letters to you do have a practical money theme to them. But if you guys do eventually marry, you will be amazed how much the money part of your lives will be influenced by your choice of spouse. So I have three rules for marriage, forged by many years observing literally thousands of them, some successes, but many failures, sad to say. Fifty percent of all marital unions in America end in divorce.

Rule #1: My number one test for *if* you should marry the person you're currently dating is "If I give him or her up, will I look back and say, 'I made a terrible mistake'?" I asked this question of myself before I married your Mimi. And I said, "Yup, I can't give her up. It will be a mistake." More than forty years later, I know it was the smartest move of my life. Think a little bit with your brain, not your heart, when you make this crucial decision.

Rule #2: If you are lucky enough to have children, make sure that at least one vacation a year is spent alone with your spouse. *No kids.* Why is this? Believe me, marriage was always a difficult institution. People change over the years, they grow intellectually at different rates. You can tell this just by your short-term dating: who appealed to you originally and who, over time, lost that certain appeal. Go away alone together, even if it's just for a long weekend. Believe me, many people forget after a while why they got married in the first place. You'll always need to reconnect with your romantic past.

Rule #3: Keep a little private place for yourself, where no one can ever get in. If you're always a little bit of a mystery to the person you marry, you will retain a certain allure for your partner. I said to your Mimi years ago, "What? I'm supposed to win you every day?" She smiled at me. "Isn't that what courtship's for?"

You can keep that courtship going if there's a small part of you that *still* has to be wooed and won.

I know that both of you have a strong romantic strain; I sense that Alyssa is a bit more intense in this regard, or Wesley's better at hiding it. I can tell by the books you read and your interests in family tales from the past. But you cannot, nor can anyone, live in romantic bubbles in the real world. Economics will always invade upon dreams, and I hope these letters will provide doses of this reality.

Your often practical Papa

In crucial decisions, use your brain first, heart second.

Believe in and Understand Cycles

Dear Alyssa and Wesley:

Please note that I never play favorites; you both get photocopies of my original letters. This week, I'm not going to tell bedtime stories or run off at the mouth. I'm just trying to underscore a few basic ideas in areas you will soon wonder about. Here's one you can take to the bank (assuming you use one that will survive these difficult economic times): *Everything* you will ever own that you hope goes up in value will fluctuate. Until the last few years, there was a feeling that real estate of all kinds—office buildings, condos, houses—would all grow in value forever. Prices plunged, people were forced out of their homes, or people abandoned them when the values dropped to points where they had negative equity.

Some years ago, we purchased a terra cotta statue

for our small garden on Beacon Hill. It was a statue of a monk, who we dubbed "Saint Spooner." The dealer from whom we bought it charged us about $1,500. He said, "This monk is special, wonderfully made, with a great expression on his face, and a bargain if you ever decide to sell it. And statues of this kind hold their value, even in tough times." I'm somewhat a cynic when it comes to so-called sure things. But we loved our monk and figured that we'd never sell it. We moved to an apartment some years after we bought Saint Spooner, and there was no room for him in our new home. Feeling sorry for all of us, he was sold for $300. The art cycle has swung back somewhat as I write this. Maybe I can buy the monk back for $2,500 or so. Just kidding.

Anything you own can go down in price from what you paid. Believe in cycles in business and in life. Cycles *always* appear, many times when you wish they wouldn't. This applies, in particular, to the house or apartment you both will eventually own. Now, I know that home ownership *is* the American dream. My dad used to say to me as he'd supervise me mowing the lawn (with a machine powered *only* by hand), "This is what the struggle is all about," as he'd survey his tiny real estate empire. Home ownership is part of the lifelong struggle in my opinion. But buying your first house or apartment is one of the two scariest decisions in life (the other being your marriage decision, assuming you two eventually make that decision). I've never known a friend or a client who wasn't terrified when purchasing his or her first house. Can I really afford it? almost everyone wonders. My tips for when this happens: Be prepared to put down 20 percent or more of the purchase price. This will give you a comfortable equity (your true ownership stake) in the property.

And, I believe in taking a thirty-year fixed mortgage, which will often give you the lowest monthly payments, allowing you more flexibility in other areas of your young lives. You can, as you make more money in your careers, pay down the mortgage amount with extra payments, anytime, with no penalties. In the real estate arena, and in many other financial matters, the simpler the better.

Back to my simple life and you to your complicated ones.

Papa

What goes around *does* come around.

All Life Is Relationships

Dear Grandchildren:

You will discover in time that all life is relationships. Assuming this is true, marriage is the closest of all one's relationships (in my opinion), and the trickiest. As noted earlier, statistics (which I generally mistrust) tell us that 50 percent of all marriages in the United States end in divorce. Believe me, money or the lack of it seems to me the single biggest cause of this.

When I was growing up, almost all my male friends had authoritarian fathers. I had only one friend whose mother worked outside of the house, and that was because of economic necessity. (The family business was going broke. She rolled up her sleeves and came in to save it.) America was a male/father-oriented society, until it all changed in the 1960s and 1970s. This old society also meant that Daddy produced the money, allocated the funds to the family, and shared almost no decisions about any of it with Mom. For almost twenty years, virtually every male client I've had who has passed away left his widow *completely* unprepared for dealing with the financial aspects of his estate. None of these male clients ever shared any money advice or business information with his spouse. The only exception, with the husband on his deathbed, was his saying, "If I die, promise you'll never sell the IBM."

Alyssa and Wesley, promise me that you'll *always* share financial ideas and thoughts, honestly and before crisis moments arise (like tumbling stock markets, or dangerous economies). From the beginning of our marriage, I talked to your Mimi nightly about markets and common sense and about my business, what made stocks go up and down. Even in my twenties, I'd say, "If I get hit by a truck tomorrow, call these two people who really have street smarts." Street smarts, practical advice, counts for so much more than dozens of words from PhDs or MBAs. I preached practicality to your grandmother in this regard. "Choose people for your team who can explain complicated issues in plain English. If I get hit by a bus and lawyers represent you, whatever documents they present to you, tell them, 'Fine. But I want you to produce for me *one* page in plain English that tells me what I just signed.'" There are many people out there in the world who seem intellectually brilliant but who have no common sense. Beware of advice from people like this, who are so sure they have all the answers. If your eventual spouse does not have a huge B.S. meter (you know very well what *that* is), make sure that *you* do.

But do talk about bills and spending together. And whether to bet on international mutual funds or domestic, or small companies, or large blue chips, or corporate bonds or tax free bonds or U.S. Treasury issues. Hash these subjects out and try not to use today's financial news as your guide to tomorrow. Most media writers on finance have never worked outside of journalism, have never worked in the corporate world, have never bought or sold stock for clients, or understood the psychological impact of the media or Internet noise around us.

And lastly, for now, never turn over important financial decisions to lawyers or accountants, unless they can explain what you are about to do in simple English paragraphs. Too many people nod their heads in agreement to people advising them, with no clue to what they are actually saying. And do not marry anyone from whom you cannot learn new ways to look at the world.

By the way, I *am* a fan of long-term relationships.

Papa

You cannot go it alone.

The Value of Stories and Bumps in the Road

Grandchildren:

I know your parents always read stories to you. I like reading stories as well and often did to your parents. But I prefer telling stories, acting them out myself. I used to tell your aunt tales of Princess Amanda who lived in a castle by the sea, in a bedroom that had a window in each of the four directions. She had elaborate breakfasts in the castle kitchen and loved tea, her pet dragon, and a knight with pink armor.

I think that stories about business and money teach lessons much better than dry textbooks or lectures about economics. Life teaches us the best lessons. And the truer the tales the more incredible they can be. Last weekend, Mimi and I had guests, old friends for many years. People can surprise you with the things they reveal, even if you've known them for ages. And, if you haven't figured this out yet, people love to talk about themselves.

You can learn a lot if you're a good listener. Here are some of the things they told us: "My father had a uniform business," our friend Bob said. "It was started by my grandfather in 1918. After college, I went to work for my dad and he started me on the factory floor for seventy-five dollars a week. He told me, 'That's your pay, which is a lot more than you're worth.' I started as a bundle boy, a human conveyer belt, carrying garments from one stitcher to another. And a stitcher was a woman who was paid per garment that she sewed, not paid much per hour. 'Piecework' was what it was called. I took care of boiler maintenance," he went on, "and I even pressed cider and let it ferment into hard stuff, and drank it with the men in the cutting room. Getting drunk with them was a rite of passage, showing I was one of the boys, not too high and mighty for *anything*. Dad rode me hard." Once Bob got rolling he didn't quit. "Debby and I married when I didn't have a pot to pee in; I'm getting beaten on psychologically, and my father says to me one day, 'You've been out on the road selling our uniforms; know the boilers, the electrical systems, the bobbins, the needles, the cans of oil. Now you're going to build us a new factory and produce products we've never produced before.'

"Debby and I were just married and she's pregnant and I'm making ninety dollars a week, that's like five hundred dollars a week today figuring inflation, twenty-four thousand dollars a year, almost poverty level. I felt I knew nothing, but Dad tossed me into it and I don't think I slept more than four hours a night for a year. Right after groundbreaking for the new factory, Dad was diagnosed with cancer and was dead in three months. I can remember feeling almost dead myself. I was staring out of my office window onto an industrial landscape, bleak, covered with snow, and I thought, I'm twenty-seven years old, with a wife and a baby on the way. It's all up to me now. I've got to do it." And Bob did it, kids. He built the family business into a major force in his industry.

I'll have another letter to you on this subject to underscore one of the great lessons of business and life: the best measure of character is how you come back from the bumps in the road that life deals to all of us. And I don't really mean the question you will ask yourselves (if you already haven't), which is, "Will I ever find someone who really loves me?" On that score, believe me—you will. For starters, I love you. (Yeah, I know, I know, Papa doesn't count.)

More on this theme of love soon.

Papa

We all need stories.

Building Your Team:
Your Lawyer

Dear Grandchildren:

There are short stories, novellas, novels, essays. Poetry. Does anyone write poems to each other anymore? So this is a really short story to make a focused point.

We live in an increasingly anonymous world, *seven billion* people on the planet, more than 300 million Americans, and growing. As you emerge into jobs after college, there is something crucial to your survival in this anonymous, scary future. You need to begin building your own team of people in what will be the most important areas in your life: medical, legal, and financial.

Since this is a quickie, let's start with picking a lawyer. You will find, as you seek your first real jobs, that you'll meet a lot of people in superior positions to you who seem to be, well, stupid. And, if not stupid, so steeped in company jargon that your eyes will roll.

But, believe me, sooner or later you will both need a lawyer, or multiple lawyers, depending on where you wander in life. You will need a lawyer for buying a house, for drawing up wills and estate plans, for corporate business, even, sadly, maybe for litigation, for people who sue you or for people you may want to sue. It's endless and frustrating. But it will be part of your new adult lives. A necessary evil. You have a chance now for some planning in this legal arena. One big principle: find and build your *own* team, *not* the team of your parents. Both of you will have classmates and friends who are going to law school. I have carried, since I graduated from college, small, pocket-sized notebooks. I have hundreds of them, all dated, full of book and story ideas, investment thoughts, little snippets of everything. They're more portable and actually more efficient than laptops; touchy-feely, too. If you buy notebooks, date them. Write down the names of classmates who seem the most solid, caring, and have the most important ingredient in this new society I see: common sense. It would help if your friends going into the law had a sense of irony, too. But common sense is the number-one quality in choosing a lawyer. I chose my main lawyer-to-be in college, because he was funny and read more books in more areas, from novels to biography to history to poetry, than anyone I knew. And, I thought, he cared about me. And would eventually care about my family. He became a wills, estates, and trust attorney. He did divorces as well. This may sound like an odd combination. But, sadly, divorce will afflict many of your friends as it has ours.

There is another good thing about having a lawyer who is a contemporary: you can grow together in your professions, deepening bonds between you. There are side benefits in choosing a lawyer early as well. They are "people persons" with wide exposure to their communities. Having an attorney with a friendship stake in you, he (or she) can be a provider for other professionals you'll need in your life. Our friend/lawyer found Mimi and me our first apartment. And he introduced me to an editor who bought and published my first novel. So always keep your eyes and ears open for tomorrow, not just today.

But have some fun today.

Your loving Papa

Build your own team.

The Value of Personal Notes

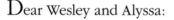

Dear Wesley and Alyssa:

The mind fills with thoughts. Words and ideas flow around us constantly. As I start this week's shout out to you, I have to add a P.S. to last week's comments on lawyers. When you are forced to deal with attorneys on any level, always take notes during your meetings. People tend to listen badly and remark after sessions with lawyers or doctors, "What did they say?" When you get your legal documents, call your lawyer and say, "Thanks for your great help. Now, if you please, send me *one* page or less, in plain English, about what we just signed off on. I can be a little dim, and I need a very short CliffsNotes style summary, so I can instantly get it."

If your lawyer is not up to expressing things in simple language for you, get one who can.

More on the correspondence subject. Let your old

Papa give you a Stone-Age tip that will pay off for you both in the digital age. Ask your parents to give you, for graduation or your birthday, personalized note cards, on good, hard stock. Wesley, you should get one hundred note cards; Alyssa, get fifty to be practical. Why fewer? Alyssa may get married someday, she may not. But, if you marry, you may choose to take your husband's name, making your cards with your maiden name or initials on them old news. Cheaper for fifty, probably. Practical, too.

So, you may ask, why note cards, when e-mail or texting is universally accepted for everything? The answer is that people of all ages *love* to receive handwritten notes. They save them. They never will forget that you sent one, because practically no one your age writes handwritten notes or letters. Making your way through an America with more than 300 million citizens is daunting. One of your biggest jobs will be: "How can I differentiate myself from the crowd?" Handwritten notes for special occasions is one big way. What are these occasions? Births, deaths, important thank-yous for above and beyond goodness to you. You two are smart and sensitive people. You'll know when to ration out these cards. And they will be treasured.

These notes can have unintended consequences that go way beyond you being original and generous. Here's a story from long ago that still resonates. I met an old lawyer in Boston, a general-purpose attorney. He could write wills, try a case in court, help you buy or sell a house, get you a divorce. He had his own small firm and every day he would go to Locke-Ober, a famous Boston restaurant, for lunch in the grill. I called him one day to ask for his stock brokerage business. And he took me to lunch to give *me* advice, buying me a martini before the food came. He threw me some small bones of business and I knocked myself out to give him great service. I even gave him advice from time to time, about markets and individual stocks, which worked out for him and he was grateful. But it was the service he most appreciated. Time passed and the older lawyer and I maintained our relationship, modest business for me, and great service from me. His wife died after a long illness. I didn't hear about it until weeks after she passed away.

I wrote him a condolence note. It was about marriage and long-term relationships and the strength of women in our lives. Happy that I had honored her life and their marriage, I never really expected any response from the lawyer. But he began referring business, sending the lawyers in his office to me for money and investment advice. The lawyers sent me *their* clients. Thirty years later, the lawyer's employees, scattered to other firms, other states, *still* refer new clients to our office, millions of dollars of relationships over many years. One simple note of condolence, and look where it led. People never forget simple acts of kindness, done in a very personal and old-fashioned way. E-mails and texting will never grab you by the heart in quite the same way.

Your ultra-personal Papa

Make it personal and it can resonate for years.

Jumping on Problems

Alyssa and Wesley:

I'm sure you'll say, "At last" when I tell you that this will be the shortest letter to you yet. But it might be one of the most important lessons, both in business and in life. You both will face many problems out there in after-college land. These problems will involve careers, business, money, relationships, all phases of your lives. They will keep you awake at night or wake you out of deep sleep. *Jump* on these problems as soon as you can, win or lose, for good or bad. Or they will fester, and in every case make the problem worse for you. *Jump* on them. Sort them out immediately. And fess up if you screwed up.

In my own life, I've made many mistakes: picking the wrong stocks for clients, hiring the wrong people for my business. It took years for me to learn to deal with mistakes quickly. Letting these mistakes linger, being reluctant to act, kept me up at night, upset my stomach, gave me headaches. My mistakes in financial planning, or with people, were not life threatening. They would not bankrupt me or put me in jail. Be decisive even if it hurts for a bit to admit you're not quite perfect. I guarantee that if you meet your problems head on and get them behind you, you will feel better and learn something in the process. And people will respect your honesty.

Yours in haste,

Papa

Bite the bullet early.

Picking a Financial Advisor

Dear Grandchildren:

I've written to you about building your own team of professionals who will be responsive to you. Let's talk about picking a financial advisor, in creative ways. Most people when searching for personal financial help almost always ask the wrong questions. They ask first of all about fees. "How much does it cost?" Cost should be your *last* question, because most money managers tend to be very similar in this department.

Here are the important things to ask, particularly because you should be seeking a long-term advisor and counselor, not someone with a good line of chatter, or B.S., if I can be a little un-grandfatherly. Don't be shocked by Papa being racy. Look at long ago pictures of almost anyone's grandparents. They were athletes, scholars, wise guys, badly behaved. They got in trouble, they made mistakes, they had sex, they fell in love. The best of grandparents pass on to the next generations their tales of many of these things, so that they flavor the imaginations of young people who carry on their blood.

I know, "Stay on the message, Grandpa." Here's what you ask a prospective financial advisor:

1. "What is your philosophy of investing? And how do you apply it to your management style?" If the person you're interviewing cannot explain this in a few simple paragraphs, keep searching for someone who can.

2. "What have been your biggest investing successes? And your biggest failures? What lessons did you learn from each?" These answers will tell you a lot about the lessons he has learned from the past, and how thoughtful he is about the future.

3. "What kind of portfolios do you build for yourself? What kinds of stocks do you own personally?"

In my experience, financial advisors have amazingly little net worth of their own. But if you're interviewing younger money managers, who haven't had years to grow wealth, ask them, "How best do you think you'll be building your own nest egg?" Ask the unusual questions of people who are going to advise you.

Feel free to ask your granddad these same questions. Maybe I'll be ready for you.

Your granddad

Unusual questions can lead to the right answers.

Be Out There in Life

Alyssa and Wesley:

Certain lessons need reinforcing. Here's a bit more on the accidental nature of life. Another half-baked theory of mine. It has to do with things like a person who walks into a room out of the blue and changes things for you forever. It can be a teacher or professor. It can be a man or woman who you never knew existed with whom you fall in love. It can be a friend or mentor who plants a seed about a career or a specific job or a graduate school choice you never considered.

But the key to "good" accidents happening to you is to be out there, forcing yourselves not to be reclusive, saying yes to invitations, reunions, charity benefits more than you say no. I had a boss once, Joe Plumeri, a great motivator of people. He is now chairman of a major sales-based insurance company that trades on the New

York Stock Exchange. Joe used to say, "I'd crawl through broken glass to get to a microphone." He could whip the troops into a frenzy and convince them that they could sell anything. And they would believe him. One of his major principles of life and business was to "go out and play in traffic." This dictum essentially reinforces the theme of "being out there" so that good accidents can happen to both of you.

There are times, of course, when neither of you will feel like being out there. You'll have the blues, be sad, disappointed, low, and not have any interest in being with people. Totally understandable. And there will be those times in business where you have to force yourself to be up, the reason being the necessity to put food on the table and to pay the rent or the mortgage. Survival is a powerful motivating force. In our family, and maybe you didn't know this, but your Mimi used to be a fashion model, among the best in the city. This was when we were dating. I told her then, "It's your dimples and personality that make you different from your competition."

She said to me, seriously, "No, it's not, it's that I worked harder than the other girls. I'd go into the modeling agency every day, even when I didn't have jobs scheduled. Every time I did this, something would come up unexpectedly. The boss would come out of her office; 'Susan,' she'd say, 'it's your lucky day; Neiman's needs someone quick to show a line to special clients.'" Just by working harder and showing up when others took days off, she'd make more money than most of her friends. She also said about this habit, "Do the unexpected. It will get you noticed and maybe set you on the trail to bigger things."

One more story about being out there and how good accidents can happen to you. You know that I've had two jobs, really, all of my adult life—one has been money management, an addictive profession, mostly because of the personal stories I've heard from thousands of people over the last fifty years. In the summer, when your grandmother is enjoying time off from my obsessions at the beach house, I go out every night, to restaurants, where I write, longhand, in notebooks. One night, several years ago, I was writing in a small neighborhood steak place, happy to scribble and take in the crowd's chatter as white noise, comforting but not hurting my concentration. A couple seated next to me were talking about loss and separation, the man counseling the woman about the obvious divorce she was going through. I eavesdropped (people love to do this, you know; me, too). When they got up to leave, the man said to me, "I know you. I was on our college humor magazine long after you. But I've read your books, and my friend needs your help." She became my client because of "right place, right time" and the accidental nature of life. It turned out that the woman was a staff writer for The *New Yorker* and was about to have *two* movies released, based on her writings. She and her restaurant companion subsequently married, and he, too, became a client.

Good accidents happen to you if you don't wait for them behind closed doors.

Your still endlessly curious grandfather

Have those good accidents.

The New Darwinian World

Alyssa and Wesley:

Good news and bad news. The bad is that you are coming into your career life in the worst economic climate since the Great Depression of the 1930s. The good news is that we are in, although most people don't get it yet, a true Darwinian period in America, where only the fittest will survive and thrive. Many people your age have no idea, yet, what I'm talking about. Part of it is that if your generation does not have the real work ethic, you might as well step aside right now and be ready for a lifetime of seeking handouts.

Thank goodness your parents always believed in summer jobs for you, and often, work on various school vacations (I should also credit your own eagerness to have some pocket money). I remember all the summers you were a camp counselor, Alyssa, teaching sailing and

God knows what else to the little angels and monsters. And Wesley, I'll never forget when you were rolling tar, repairing roofs for that real estate developer with your friend, who would show up for the job barefoot and hungover. He was fired even though his dad was the real estate guy's best friend. "Life is work," my father told me often, "whether you want to hear this or not."

We live in a society where the first thing people will ask upon meeting you is, "And what do you do?" We're defined in America by what we do, for better or worse. Your grandmother hated this question. In the 1970s, women really started to pour into the workforce, and at parties these workers always questioned the new women they met. "And what do *you* do?" they all asked.

"I'm a neurosurgeon," your Mimi would answer. "That usually shut them up," she'd tell me, "since no one really knew anything about neurosurgery."

When your grandparents grew up, people tended to stay in one community where you knew most of your neighbors. Life was relatively simple. People married and stayed in these communities. They all listened to the same radio programs. When television arrived they all watched the same shows. *Your Hit Parade* played the top songs in America and everyone sang the same tunes. There were no birth control pills. Major league sports existed in only a handful of cities. I could go on and on, but you get the picture. Now we have limitless choices, attention spans of seconds, not hours, and an extremely fragmented sense of community. It makes for a society in a constant state of anxiety. Why pound on these points? Because you two have to navigate this fractured world, and you will need to find a few centers for yourselves to cope with it all. By centers, I mean a few core beliefs you can focus on to find your way. I'll tell you three of mine—in life, business, and investment matters—as examples of my bedrock principles:

1. I believe in, and always fall back on, my sense of the absurdity of life, the foolish, amazing, unpredictable qualities of human nature. If you're prepared for the absurd, you'll be better prepared for the bumps in life.

2. Rely on people who are practical, who believe in cutting through bureaucracy and red tape. These are the folks with what is still called "street smarts." I trust the advice from these people much more than I trust academic brilliance, typified by the ivory tower mentality of professors and economists. Believing in people with too many graduate degrees after their name can often be a trap that leads us down paths of disaster in business and government affairs.

3. When you're out in your careers, go to as few meetings as you possibly can. Have coworkers

give you the highlights in ten minutes or less after the meetings. When you run meetings eventually, hammer away at the important points in simple language. And if you schedule a meeting to last an hour, finish it fifteen minutes early. Everyone who works for you will appreciate it, and the really good employees will say, "Great. More time for productivity."

Love,
Your somewhat cynical Papa

Street smarts mean more than genius.

Collectibles

Grandchildren:

Have you ever watched the TV program *Antiques Roadshow*? It's somewhat addictive; you can see the stuff people inherit or blunder into buying and how sometimes the junk you possess for various reasons can turn into gold. I've briefly seen your bedrooms over the years, Wesley's with posters of Bobby Orr and Larry Bird (I like you caring about legends gone by, even though I'm not sure you ever saw them play). Alyssa, you've always been much more romantic than your brother, nostalgic for eras you never saw, the 1930s, 1940s, 1950s. I know you have fashion photos, torn from *Vanity Fair, Vogue*. And pictures of movie stars long gone: Gary Cooper, Bette Davis, Hepburn, Jack Lemmon (you once told me you really liked him because when he was a young actor, he brought in extra money playing the piano in bars). The point is that you displayed images reflecting your passions and interests. From this premise is where successful collecting sprouts.

I love art of all kinds. Our houses and my office walls are covered with cartoons, photographs, watercolors, oils, serigraphs, pochoir (look it up). It's all a helter-skelter, eclectic muddle with none of it cohesive. Just a bunch of things, mostly with lots of color, we've assembled over the years. All of it dear to us. Every piece with a story. That's the point. Everything on our walls has a story, about a time in our lives, or by artists who were friends. In my case, every time a book of mine was published, I'd take some of the writing money and buy a painting that I thought reflected the theme of the book. The two nineteenth-century portraits of a merchant husband and his American Indian wife in our dining room were bought when *Smart People* was published in 1979. When I view the portraits, it reminds me of the thought and effort I put into writing that book. This is all fun for me, but not the way collections that really grow in value are created.

Since these letters should be bedrock lessons about money and life, I want the advice to be about maximizing your assets, not strictly upon living the good and just life. As in my concentration theory of building wealth in the stock market, extraordinary collecting focuses hard on a period or a school of artists, unless it's stamps and coins, which can be all over the lot, but focused in other special ways.

One great example I've seen: An older client of mine, as a very young lawyer, was taken along to Amsterdam to be the junior attorney on a law firm matter. He was to do all the grunt work. At the time, he had a young wife and child and was making six thousand dollars a year. During a lunch break, he wandered the Amsterdam streets, going into several bookstores and galleries. He picked through a rack of Dutch master drawings, some selling for about twenty-five dollars. He was intrigued by owning something by Rembrandt for so little and fell in love with the Dutch subject matter and execution. And he could afford it, even on his meager salary. This simple beginning led to a lifelong passion for these drawings for both my client and his wife. After thirty-five years of collecting, they gave half of their holdings to a college museum, which valued the donation at more than $20 million.

If I were starting today, I'd probably concentrate on drawings and paintings that were satirical in nature, scenes of people displaying humor or a sense of the absurd in life. In other words, pick a theme. If it's to be fun and games, and all over the lot, stay with Bobby Orr or Bogart and Bacall photos. But make sure that whatever hangs on your walls, or sits in albums or book-shelves or on shelves, has personal meaning to both of you. Have fun with collecting.

Your loving packrat Papa

In collecting, focus on a theme.

Accountants

Dear Grandchildren:

From the sublime to the ridiculous: a letter about collecting what you love and enjoy to a letter about accountants. But I want to touch on every business aspect of your adult lives. This includes building your team of the people you'll need to take care of your basic needs. You will both need accountants. It is a waste of your time and energy to do it yourselves. My sister, who has a relatively simple tax life selling wine to retail customers, uses the national tax preparers H&R Block. Fast for her. And cheap, relative to private accountants. She pays about $200 a year. Your Mimi and I paid $2,500 last year for a fairly complex return. I have a client who pays six figures for his personal return. His forms fill five standard moving boxes.

Another longtime client of mine is a street-smart cynic with his opinions backed by years of running various businesses. Here's what he told me years ago on the subject of accountants. "Friends would call me over the years and say, 'My accountant says...' I'd say stop. Never take investment advice from your accountant. Think about it—did you ever meet a rich accountant in your entire life?" Whenever I tell anyone this story, they laugh. Of course they've never met a rich accountant.

So forget financial advice from the people who push the pencils (or the cursors) on your tax returns. Take tax advice only. And my last dictum for this relationship is: Ask your potential tax advisors if they have had strong experience dealing with the Internal Revenue Service representing their clients. Accountants should appear *for* you in any audit of your tax returns. They will not be emotional the way you would be. (I know, I once threw an inkwell against a wall during an audit of our return. It was not a good idea.) Pick an accountant who has common sense and a talent for people to defend you against government bureaucracy: a subtle person with a sense of irony and politics.

Love,
Your mathematically challenged,
sometimes hotheaded Papa

**Get the returns done, forget the
financial advice.**

Real Estate

Grandchildren:

Both of you grew up in relatively stable homes. I say "relatively" because every family, I think, is a soap opera of its own.

But each of you lived with your parents and siblings in very few houses, moving only twice. Your folks each sold your first houses at very good profits and real estate seemed like a great investment to them. Their current homes have also appreciated, but nowhere near the rise in prices of their first homes. Recent years have proved to almost everyone that home values do not just go up and up forever. They fluctuate just like stocks, the price of gold, interest rates, and the value of baseball trading cards.

There is one big difference in real estate, however. You can see the prices of stocks every minute on a stock exchange. Things you may collect or want to collect you can find on eBay or other Internet sites where buyers and sellers meet. While you can check approximate home values in your neighborhood on various websites, guessing games mean nothing. I can believe that some stock of mine has an intrinsic value of $50. But if it's $25 and I'm forced to sell it to raise money, all I'll get today is $25.

The American dream used to be home ownership. For your generation it might be "when my college loans are paid off." More people are renting houses and apartments today than ever before in my memory. For years, Americans said, "Our houses can only go one way: up." Wrong. *Everything* fluctuates in value. And the trap in real estate is that you cannot sell a house like a stock and get your money overnight. Real estate is mostly an illiquid investment. Mimi and I had our house on Beacon Hill for sale for more than a year, at the same time owning the apartment we were moving into. Not a great feeling, having two mortgages, one of which we felt was bleeding us every month. Even the smartest of us get what I call the "night sweats" over all kinds of things. "What if we can *never* sell the house?" I'd ask myself in the dangerous hours, three to four in the morning. That's when our anxieties seem to pour in, no matter what our age. And we can all get jammed up in life, no matter how smart we are or how well we think we have planned.

One of the happiest days of my life was when we finally sold that house and paid off the large debt. And I thought I was somewhat of a cool customer (if grandfathers can ever be called "cool"). Well, we all delude ourselves. Just promise me, you two, that when you catch yourselves in self-delusion, you'll laugh about it.

I have a lot of prejudices about various things, as you've noticed. But I prefer to take the longest fixed mortgage terms possible, thirty years. And pay the lowest monthly payment. Debt is a head game much of the time. You'll learn what you're comfortable with. Everyone I've ever met in the real estate business, particularly the most successful ones, treat debt either as their friend or as a petty annoyance, like a summer cold. I like small monthly payments, if the interest rate is favorable, so that I can do other things with the money that does not go toward the mortgage.

Like buying liquid growth stocks. Or planning for a special trip, places you've never been. You can always put extra dollars against your mortgage, pay it off earlier, with no penalties. I say this as a person who basically hates debt and has seen people in the stock market wiped out by margin calls. They bought stock on credit, putting up 50 percent, typically, of the purchase price. As stocks dropped, the investment firm called and asked for more collateral. If the customer had no cash to bring in or other securities to offer, the investment firm would sell them out of their holdings. This was often done at desperation prices, wiping out the entire investment. Too much debt scares me. But long-term mortgages, which you pay down with monthly payments, can be both prudent and wise.

Should you experiment with real estate investments for profit? Sure. You'll learn a lot about yourselves and the ways of the world. Just beware of the debt side in these adventures. In the mid 1980s, Mimi and I bought a small house, "on spec," to speculate and invest. I thought it would be a sure thing, an oceanfront development with a nine-hole golf course. I paid for it in full and intended to rent it to tenants and eventually sell it for a long-term capital gain (which you get if you hold an investment for more than one year).

You will never really know yourselves until you put your real money on the line. Mimi and I held this property for ten years, and it was rented to various people all that time. We learned a lot. For one, even nice people will trash rental property. For another, we hated the pain in the neck of renters, many of whom would call at midnight to say, "The toilet's plugged" or "Do you have a corkscrew?" You never know until you're in the experience. We sold the house after ten years and I figured out we annualized our investment at about 2 percent—less than money market funds paid then and with much more aggravation. So no bricks and mortar for me. Give me one hundred shares of Johnson & Johnson any day. They don't call me in the middle of the night. They pay me dividends. And they make Band-Aids.

Know thyselves, Alyssa and Wesley. None of us are good at everything.

Papa

**Trees do not grow to the skies.
Everything fluctuates.**

Insurance

Alyssa and Wesley:

Could anything be as boring as insurance? Probably not. That's why you'll probably say to each other, "Is Papa getting bored with writing to us?" Nope. Not bored, but this week it's almost like a tweet. The best real lessons in life, other than learning from your own mistakes, come almost in sound bites, backed up by selected anecdotes from someone's practical experience. Here are the three simple keys to any insurance you'll ever buy in your lives:

1. Tell the insurance person calling on you, "No canned speeches, please. I can tell when you've memorized a script. Plain talk only."
2. Because of the Internet, whether you're buying a car or plane tickets or insurance, it's easy to get quotes from all over on whatever coverage you

want. So you only need to know if the insurance agent and her agency have clout! Clout with the claims adjusters who will determine how much you're entitled to in the claims process. And clout in getting you proper amounts of insurance for tricky requests you might have. For instance, after Hurricane Katrina, it became really tough and really expensive to get insurance in areas near water. For our beach house, which you both love and cherish, I couldn't get coverage for anywhere near the replacement value of the property. Our small local agency had no clout with insurance carriers. We had to fire them and go with our Boston agent, a street-smart veteran, who got us expanded coverage at lower cost than our local person. Our street-smart guy had *clout*.

3. You want "service, service, service" from your insurance person. They should check in once a year and ask, "Any changes in your life since I saw you last?" This question will almost always trigger a response. Because *every* year things will change in your life. And you do need protection in various ways, new ways like identity theft, for instance.

"Service, service, service" is good for your agent's business. And, in an increasingly anonymous world, it will be good for both of you.

I still hate the idea of insurance, but it's part of life "after school."

Love,
Practical Papa

It's service, service, service that you'll need.

Lessons in Selling Stock

Grandchildren:

I've made a major financial mistake in my life, I think blinded by my own natural optimism. I don't know why this is, but no ever seems to get our attention in warning us about pitfalls. It's as if we only really learn by the experience of our own errors. Anyway, I'm going to tell you about a big blunder of mine. (I also hate to tell anyone specifics about personal money matters. My dad always told me that you should never count anyone else's money because, "You'll always be wrong. In both directions." I think that's true.)

In any event, over a period of more than ten years, I had accumulated enough shares in Citibank to make it my largest personal stock holding, worth multiple seven figures; enough to allow most Americans to retire forever to the good life. I accumulated this holding mainly because I believed in the CEO, who had created for me, over twenty years, most of my net worth, through his tough mindedness and his visions of the future. I believed in him and bet on these visions. He was approaching his seventieth birthday in 2002 and I said to your grandmother, "If he retires, we're going to sell all of our stock. Without him, I don't really trust anyone who comes after. Remind me I said this." But he didn't retire and the dividend kept being raised annually, and we were receiving more than $100,000 from this dividend alone. The boss did not want to retire, he loved the action, and power is addictive. But he was eventually forced out and he retired.

"You said you were going to sell the stock if he retired," your Mimi reminded me.

"Citibank is one of the great brands in the world," I answered. "It'll muddle along, and the dividend pays us a small fortune." I never believed the dividend would be cut. The chief financial officer said publicly that there was no need to cut it. Plus, I liked the new CEO. I thought he was smart, and he certainly was funny. Human. And he liked me. We can be blinded by flattery from the seats of power. Be aware of this in your business lives.

Being in the trenches daily, advising people on their money decisions and their lives, I was oblivious to the damage being caused to the banking system by Wall Street corporate management and their decisions. My

Citibank stock melted down, from more than $55 a share to under $1 at the lowest point. Now I'm in the process of digging out from the financial tsunami and getting to the number that means freedom.

Big lessons in all this?

1. Stick to your discipline, and don't be a financial pig. If you make a decision, like mine, to sell if your leader leaves the company, then stay with the plan. Of course, my argument that the dividend would be preserved was flawed as well. It was eventually cut to zero.

2. Buying anything is easy. But selling something of value is the hardest part of any trade. My take on this is to pick a reasonable number, not a pie in the sky target, the minute you buy a stock. "What profit would I be comfortable with?" is my question to myself. Whenever that stock hits that target, I will immediately sell either a third or a half and seek a new target for selling the rest.

3. I try to give myself three good reasons why I should continue to own the position. This is what I also do when I'm thinking of buying any stock. And I ask new clients to do this as well when they come to me with stock they already own. If they cannot give me three good reasons to own, time to sell it. Yes, markets are emotional. But

there are times you must force yourself to be cold-blooded about them.

Love,
Your Papa, who is still making mistakes
but at least fessing up about them

Always set a target price.

Asking the Unusual
Questions

Wesley and Alyssa:

This may seem like an odd letter. What do unusual questions have to do with money and business? As I've told you many times, I lived for the first five years of my life in my maternal grandparents' house. My mother had three brothers and a sense of humor. That aura of the ridiculous ruled the household. I grew up surrounded by laughter. My uncle Howard was the youngest, a very profane man who believed that rules were for other people. Not admirable, I'll admit. But he was a character who went two years to medical school, ended up manufacturing maternity dresses, and was in World War II, starting in the army as a private, stringing wires on telephone poles, and ended up as an ensign in the navy. He used to say to me, when I was five years old, "How's the back of your mind?" And he'd tell people, "Fine. Take vitamins and yoga. And exercise five times a week. It's all worthless and lets you live three weeks longer than you would have. It's either in the genes or it isn't." Right before he died at eighty-nine years old, having smoked a pipe for almost eighty of those years and abused himself terribly with fatty foods and sugar. "Remember," he told me, "see the world through ironic glasses and always search for ways to separate yourself from the crowd." I try to ask questions no one else seems to ask to get unusual answers from people, to open them up to feeling comfortable and responding. Here are a few examples of this:

In this increasingly anonymous world, people seem more disconnected than ever. And this in the era of constant communications. Often when I call people on business matters, I hear a response (when you actually reach a *person*) like "Mr. or Ms. Parsons is not available, what is the nature of your call?"

"Please tell Ms. Parsons it's John Spooner and I'm calling about her emotional future." I *always* get a call back. It's made them curious.

Another truth about people: Most of us cannot resist tales of our childhood, simpler times, even if they were not such good memories. I've found that these can be magic words when I meet new people in business: "What were you like in high school?" Anyone I've ever asked this question universally smiles and gushes forth the most amazing stories. And with honesty as well. You can tell a lot about character from this exercise.

Last example, and one that I find can teach you a lot about people. I ask every potential new client and everyone I'm with at small business gatherings: "What's your favorite all-time book, and your favorite movie?" This is a very quick way to interpret how people are likely to react to profits, losses, disappointments in life. For instance, here's a quickie thumbnail of your Papa: My favorite all-time book is *The Great Gatsby* by F. Scott Fitzgerald. This marks me, I think, as an incurable romantic and a sucker for fictional tales that mirror the American soul. One of my favorite two movies remains *Casablanca*, with Humphrey Bogart and Ingrid Bergman, which reinforces my romantic strain and also the idea of the tough American male maverick, a role I also relish (except for the "tough" part). Tied with *Casablanca* is *Animal House*, a wicked satire, and so smart in many ways. So my favorite book and movies instantly tell you a lot about me. And also about my hot buttons that smart people could push if they needed or wanted to interest me. Wesley, you don't want to hear about a romantic grandfather, a contradiction in terms you might say. Alyssa, you and I have talked in the past about romance, so no news to you.

I shared this concept several years ago with Chuck Prince, then CEO of Citibank, as a way to get disparate segments of the business, disparate managers in different divisions to perhaps bond with one another through more human interactions. Swapping favorite books and movies would personalize relationships. Common ground might be found. Prince bought the idea and it morphed into the "One Citi" initiative. He even gave me credit for it; the "Spooner Protocol," he called it. Unfortunately, the financial meltdown signaled the end of Prince's reign and the end of the protocol. But it has worked in many personal ways that I know can be useful to my grandchildren. Try it.

Love,
Your still romantic yet irreverent Papa

Make yourself memorable.

News, the Media, and the Dangers of "They"

Grandchildren:

In these anxious times, with you two very shortly getting ready to join America's full-time employment ranks, here's some words about worry and the news that daily swirls around all of us. Neither of you, I know, is applying to medical school or law school after college. And so far, neither of you has mentioned any other graduate school as yet. So it looks like the job market, competing against all your fellow recent graduates. People are going to say to you, "Jobs are impossible to get; no one's hiring. Now's a terrible time to start a business, go to Wall Street, go to Hollywood, etc." This is all bull, negative energy, and you both must screen it out.

It's fine to be an information junkie. Just don't assume that because something is in print it's gospel. Very few financial writers ever ran anyone's money.

We are surrounded by news and opinion every day, all day; news from networks, cable, the Internet, bloggers, tweets, phones and text, office gossip, rumors. Everything but the Dixie cup and string fake phones of my youth and the walkie-talkies of days gone by.

As for jobs, no matter what the business climate, companies of all kinds are always looking for talented people who are full of energy and desire. They are looking for "fire in the belly." No matter how terrible stock markets are, I would hire such a person in a heartbeat. Never listen to what "they" say. Who are "they" anyway? I wish I knew.

People in business and active in life do process the news and the rumors. But they have to make their own businesses prosper. They, and you starting your careers, must focus on productivity. You must pour your energies into being creative, working hard, and prospering. It doesn't matter what "they" say. Concentrate on what *you* say and do.

Love,
Your Papa, who is rooting for you both, every day

Who are "they" anyway?

Letter to Alyssa

Alyssa:

"This Bud's for you," as the old Budweiser beer ad said. It's for your eyes only, unless you choose to share it with Wesley. Children will accept advice from friends, strangers, teachers, coaches. But from parents? An old line is "The definition of an expert is 'someone from fifty miles outside of town.'" And the oldest sayings about human nature, going back to the Bible, seem eternally true.

I know I have a lot of "woman" in me. And I consider this to be a very lucky thing. By a lot of "woman," I mean that I have a lot of strong female friendships and more than three hundred woman clients, all over the world, from California to Arizona, Texas, Florida, Ohio, New Mexico, London, Illinois, and Malaysia, not just in the Northeast. And I think creativity helps. I started out to be a novelist, and, in my view, this means you better be detached, sympathetic, and understanding of your characters, male *and* female. Women have always confided in me, sensing a friend, I hope. Since I've created women characters in my books, maybe I have some valid observations for my dear granddaughter.

This week, the reports tell us, women, for the first time in U.S. history, exceeded the number of men in the workplace. I know that you have every expectation of having a career outside of the home. I hope that you will be married someday and that you will have children. And, I know, we live in a society where sometimes it's difficult even to define relationships in any traditional way.

I believe that the ideal life has two elements to it: (1) You should love where you show up for work each day, whatever you do, and (2) You should have someone who meets you at home every evening. Someone who you can talk to about the activities of the day. Sounds simple. But I know hundreds of people who have one of these things and very few who have both.

Always try to have a best woman friend. Women are much more honest with each other than the guys are. You will need someone as a confidante with whom you will never share a bed.

Always know what your own money is doing, and work at understanding it. Seek advice from many sources in this regard. Do not have knee-jerk reactions about

money managers like, "I can only use another woman."
Pick the best person for this job regardless of gender,
someone who is practical and speaks not in clichés, but
in simple, common sense terms. A fair test phase for a
new financial advisor is three years. If there has been
no progress in growth of your money, rethink it then.
But, don't second-guess these people unless something
seems terribly wrong. Second-guessing handcuffs these
managers. You're paying them a fee for what *they* do,
not for sticking your two cents in.

Force yourself to be curious, Alyssa. My mother was
talented, but unfortunately, lazy. The family joke was
that "Mom never saw noon in her life." An exaggera-
tion. Let's just say she was slow to get started. I think
she had dreams of a different life. But she soldiered on,
playing the hand she was dealt. A talented artist, she
never worked at it or poured herself into her work. I tell
you this because, even though you don't want preaching
from me, you'll suddenly say about your birthdays "The
big three-oh," then "The big four-oh." Time is a thief.
Check out adult education classes in your community
and sample areas you know nothing about, like classic
Italian movies or legal reasoning. You will go through
different phases of your adult life and, if you marry and
have children, you'll discover pieces of your character
you never knew existed. The more you try to use both

sides of your brain, the creative and the practical, the better prepared you will be for all of these phases.

When or if you have a home of your own and you are in a marriage, remember something I've told you in the past. Every single night I came home from work, over the course of our lives together, your Mimi would greet me at the door with an enormous smile as if, to her, I was the most important person in the world. It made me so happy regardless of the toughness of the day. Telling this story reminds me of advice a wonderful woman friend of mine told me. She has been named many times to various lists, including the 100 Best Women Executives in America. She said about marriage, "If you're in a high-pressure job, never be a pain in the butt around the house." I second the motion.

This won't be the last letter only to you. I know that women rule, but, in the light of full disclosure, I'll give Wesley a few solitary pats on the back as well.

Love,
Your talkative, opinionated Papa

Don't be a pain in the butt around the house.

The Eight-Hundred-Pound Gorilla

Alyssa and Wesley:

If you ever run a business, whether it is manufacturing mattresses or managing money, beware of the eight-hundred-pound gorilla, otherwise known as "the major client." I have watched any number of so-called hotshots over the years in the investing game. These were people who were raking in big fees or commissions, but from a handful of really well-heeled clients, not from a broad base of business, scattered all over the country or the world. In every case in my memory, the hotshots with the giant clients eventually lost them and most of the hotshots disappeared from sight.

One of my good friends produced fabric for furniture of all kinds. At some point General Motors became a client, and my friend made seat covers for their cars. GM dominated my friend's business, demanding more and more from them, in fabric and in time. My friend said to me then, "GM is killing me. We're making more money than we ever have, but so many of our old-time smaller customers are leaving us, our base is shrinking. What's going to happen when the giant gets tired of us, or squeezes us on prices, or just demands too much?" Sure enough, GM at some point fired my friend's company and they went through terrible times, ending eventually in bankruptcy.

So beware of the wonderful business relationship that becomes so important to you that you neglect older, solid, loyal customers because you have no time. Remember, big money, like General Motors, is fickle money. Really rich investment clients are the same— fickle. They move with the wind and where they think the hot money is moving. Loyalty changes in the blink of an eye. Remember this in your own business lives.

Love,
Your ever-vigilant Papa

Big money is fickle money.

Wesley, My Boy

Wesley:

I'm proud to be your grandfather, proud you have fire in your belly, determined not to drift in life but to embrace it and throw yourself into it.

Let's get the marriage piece of my rant out early. I married later than most of my college classmates, which meant I was just shy of thirty. Most of my class (all men) married upon graduation, and married whomever they were dating at the end of senior year. They were all *kids*. I thought I needed a little more experience. In fact, I think I was both terrified about marrying and selfish as well. Nice to know thyself. We fool ourselves endlessly about ourselves, and it's probably healthy to admit our qualities that are not so attractive.

Here's my honest standard for marrying: I was not enjoying the investment business and wanted only to be a novelist. At the time I had been dating your grandmother for about a year and the pressure was mounting to tie the knot. Your Mimi was and is a very independent person, and she was constantly being asked out by all sorts of men. This, of course, drove me nuts. Then something lucky happened. I had a chance to escape for two weeks, with no heavy lifting and time to think without being in an office. I had to go to two weeks of Army Reserve training in upstate New York. I've told you that I was the unit historian, boondoggle of all boondoggles, walking around as if I knew what I was doing. My sole responsibility was writing a daily paragraph about our activities. Most of each day, I took a truck to a nearby lake, worked on a novel about army life, swam, sunbathed (an admirable thing in those days), and did my paragraph in about fifteen minutes. And I thought about Mimi. Halfway into a week of this retreat I had the breakthrough moment.

She was an adult. She approached problems with common sense. And she was funny, too, with an ironic twist to her humor. Forty-three years later I know I was right. Sorry I can't tell you what your Mimi's defining moment was. She's not writing these letters. Ask her.

Now about careers. Here's my big headline about this: You Never Know. And whatever you think you're planning for, it will probably never quite work out as you've planned. It may be much better, or it may be worse, but life seldom delivers what you predict.

Odd things often drive us on to results we never considered. Anger can be motivating, or the intense desire to prove someone wrong. Years ago, beginning to work for my dad, and hating it, I was living at home, which made it even worse. I had started writing my first novel, late at night and on weekends, single-spaced, on my old Smith Corona portable typewriter. I thought that when— not if—my first novel was published, I'd be set free, and I could quit the money game. One night, I heard my father say to my mom, from their bedroom, "He'll never write a book; he'll never finish one. It's a pipe dream." That conversation drove me on. It drove me to what I thought would be freedom.

In recent years, I knew of a young woman, the daughter of a client, whose father fired her from a family business because he thought the young woman would eventually run it into the ground. The daughter, incredibly bitter, had a family trust fund. She took off for travel around the world. And, years later, she's still doing it. No job, no intention of getting one. She was a potentially talented young woman and has wasted her life. The family, out of guilt, has replenished the fund, enabling her. A sad story in my view. I know, Wesley, you're saying, "I get it, Papa. Put my shoulder to the wheel. Be the grit in the oyster. How we handle the bumps in life is the true measure of character."

And you'd be right, Wesley. Just don't look back on anything and say, "Wudda, cudda, shudda—*didn't*."

As for families, I may be shocking you, but my advice on the matter—love them, of course. But don't let family suck the oxygen out of you.

From the grandfather who loves you, knowing that we'll both survive these revelations

You never know.

Wills, Trusts, and Estates—Planning Ahead

Dear Alyssa and Wesley:

Why would I even raise these issues? Neither of you are on the career path yet. Part of the reason is to get all of this stuff down for you early, as you're starting your new journey. Many of the tips of the trade I'm trying to pass on to you are not just my observations over many years, they are bits of wisdom from various experts, who have been, and are, important in my life. Here's practical, down and dirty commentary from our personal wills, estates, and trusts lawyer. He is also a family counselor who cares about our family, including both of you. He's also practical and funny, an unusual combination.

I have to go to Palm Beach to meet with my estate lawyer. He doesn't live there, but he does love to wander in places where the rich and famous go to play.

"Great estate lawyers are voyeurs," he tells me. "They never participate in life; they observe it."

My estate lawyer's name is Peter, and he answers all four of my requirements for people who are on my personal team:

1. He was originally recommended to me by very smart friends.
2. Peter is quirky, a character, whose main talent in life is his understanding of human nature.
3. The syndicated columnist Ellen Goodman told me years ago that she wanted people working for her who are obsessive-compulsive, who are workaholics. "They need to take care of me before they take care of themselves. They can't help it. Horrible way to live, but great for the people they care for."

   Peter is obsessive-compulsive. He dates when he is in Palm Beach, and he always dines in the same restaurant so the service will be assured. He keeps several Ferragamo scarves with the bartender, whom he has taken care of in advance. Peter sits at the bar with each new date, and if the first round of drinks goes well, he will say, "This is a magic bar for the right people." He signals the bartender. "See what happens here, if you have the look." Then the bartender produces the beautifully wrapped package containing the Ferragamo scarf. "Don't dump on the poor wills and estates lawyer," Peter has said to me. "Yes, it's corny. But the attention to detail is like being a set designer. That's why people come from all over the world to have me do their estates."

4. He is younger than I am. You have to start developing experts who are at least a few years your junior. You want people on your team who are very much in the hunt professionally, not close to retirement.

Over the last several years, Peter has made his estate plan principles very clear. I'm sure the practical side of you will find these valuable:

1. If you are truly rich, estate planning is done by the accumulation of control and power, not through the accumulation of assets.

2. Choose that person for your trustee or executor whom you trust most in the world. It is an act of conferring power, and it becomes the ultimate act of love for a man to give his wife that power.

3. A client should never make his lawyer the trustee; there are too many conflicts of interest. And never duplicate the roles of the people who serve you. Your trustee, lawyer, and money manager should all be separate people.

4. Always pay your lawyer by the hour, never by the size of the estate.

5. The biggest mistake you can make is making a corporate lawyer your trustee. Think about the word "trustee": he or she is someone you should trust completely because often a trustee's primary responsibility is to hire and fire other professionals who are working in your behalf.

6. Never make a bank or institution your trustee. They charge big fees, and they cannot organize toilet paper. Furthermore, never make any professional your executor. Make it a *personal* relationship.

7. If you want to live like the rich people live, start signing your name as trustee, as opposed to owner, early in life. People of substantial wealth have their own names on nothing.

8. My number one goal is "Do no harm." Lawyers have a penchant for doing more harm than good: I'm sorry, but it's true. Don't make it worse. Most lawyers think they know the answers. The client knows the answers—your lawyer needs to know the questions.

9. When you hire a lawyer to do a will or trusts for you, make sure he or she is practical. So often estate lawyers give you their last client's plan: it's a nice pair of shoes, but it doesn't fit you. Get referrals when you search for a lawyer, and if common sense seems to be lacking, always go elsewhere.

Why do I always hammer on the "common sense" theme? In a world with more than seven *billion* people, that quality means more than anything.

Your practical Papa

Make sure, above all, that the lawyer has common sense.

Beware of Genius

Alyssa and Wesley:

This may seem like an odd subject. But what I have to say may save you a lot of teeth gnashing as your careers progress, and I'll bet it will save you money as well. Here are a few stories that underscore what I'm getting at:

If you give counsel and advice to people, you'd better have a reasoned game plan for every market condition, and you'd better have a sense of history that equips you to have clues about the future. One of my key financial insights was identifying what I call the "Emperor's New Clothes Syndrome." People who exhibit this syndrome very often cause enormous damage when allowed to run amok in the real world. Here's an illustration: I met Alan Greenspan before he became chairman of the Federal Reserve Board. He was speaking at a company retreat for the top 5 percent of our sales force and the management team that included the former Citigroup CEO Sandy Weill. The three-day event was held on Marco Island, Florida, with Greenspan delivering the keynote address.

At the last night's black-tie dinner, Greenspan seemed totally oblivious to his audience of half-drunk stockbrokers with celebration on their minds. He spoke for almost twenty-five minutes. A friend at our table said as he droned on, "Do you think he's at the wrong meeting? The American Society of Embalmers is in the next ballroom." Our regional manager, I noticed, was whispering in the ear of his female table partner, coming dangerously close, I thought, to kissing it. People were fleeing the tables, heading for the open bars. Another friend stopped behind my chair and leaned down. "We paid this guy money?" he said. "What the hell language is he speaking? Esperanto?"

"Mr. Greenspan will take a few questions," one of our management team then said from the podium when Greenspan's totally incomprehensible speech finally came to an end.

"He'll probably be fired Monday for hiring him," someone said about our guy on the stage. Another voice said, "Well, it takes a con to know a con" about Greenspan.

I asked the first question.

"Mr. Greenspan," I said. "This is a room full of stock-brokers. We live and die each day on the movement of markets. This is a two-part simple question. One: Given the state of the economy, would you be a buyer of common stocks today? And two: If you would be a buyer, what sort of companies and/or sectors would you choose?"

Those were direct questions. Alan Greenspan rattled on with answers, obtuse and obscure, never answering either one. Our flunky thanked him and he exited, probably off to the paying teller's window. People bitched to me the rest of the night about Greenspan's appearance. Management basically threw up their hands. One of our vice chairmen said, "What can I tell you; he was supposed to be really great."

The next day, my wife and I were flying back to Boston. A puddle jumper was to take us to Miami, and from there a regular flight home. There was Greenspan as well, climbing into the small plane ahead of us, brief-case clutched to his bosom. When everyone was in their seats, I said to my wife, "Greenspan's three seats in front of us. I am going to ask my questions again."

"Don't bother him, he's probably working," she said.

"That's ridiculous," I said. "The firm didn't get their money's worth; let's see if he's more relaxed now."

"Well," she said, "if anyone can make him nervous, it's you." I slipped down the aisle and stopped next to Alan Greenspan, who was shuffling through papers in his briefcase. I leaned down, "Excuse me, Mr. Greenspan." He immediately attempted to cover his papers with his hands and arms as if he were Silas Marner jealously protecting his stash of gold. "I'm not the cat burglar," I said. "I'd just like to know what you *really* think."

He continued to play cover-up. "Can't you see I'm working?" he said, extremely annoyed. I just shook my head, muttered "Pitiful," and retreated to my seat.

"Learn anything?" my wife asked me, smiling.

"Yeah," I said. "Sometimes you pull the curtain aside and there's no one there." *If someone cannot explain his economic concepts to you in several simple paragraphs, then you should view those concepts as probably being dangerous to your financial health.* Greenspan's policy of lower interest rates at any cost helped drive Wall Street to leverage risky bets as high as 20 or 30 to 1. Leverage and debt, for government and people, sooner or later are killers, regardless of when they appear in history.

Here's a more recent encounter with brilliance. Your Mimi and I went to a dinner and lecture a week ago, the attraction being a well-known economist who was to speak on financial collapse and the economic chaos of the last several years; he would also discuss his views of the future. For forty-five minutes or so he went on about the causes of the meltdown and then predicted a long, difficult economic road ahead with government, in his opinion, unwilling to do what it would take to get the country on track. Eventually, he paused and asked for any questions.

I raised my hand first. After thanking the professor for his insights, I said, "Almost everyone in this room is either retired or almost retired. There is only one question on all of their minds," I continued, "and that one question is, What do I do with my money?" The brilliant economist responded for about five minutes about why he couldn't answer the question and then called on someone else.

So-called brilliant minds certainly contributed to the financial and economic meltdown of the last several years. On a very personal note, they also indirectly contributed to perhaps a tough time for finding jobs for young people like you. So as you get older, pay attention to people who are not necessarily academically brilliant. I've mentioned before that I was allowed to skip second-year algebra in high school because I was so inept. I took art instead. My friends laughed when I went into the money business. And yet a Boston magazine a few years ago picked me as the city's number one financial advisor. What's the moral here? Please give me people in my life who don't preach from on high, but who can solve day-to-day problems in practical ways and who know more about people than pie in the sky models.

Love,
Your Papa, who wants people to get to the point

Never be intimidated by people with graduate degrees.

A Business Quickie

Dear Grandchildren:

I believe that if you live long enough, you actually get smarter. Not because of brain power so much as the accumulated number of setbacks and disappointments that all of us experience.

The last two letters were long. Occasionally I have time on my hands and desperately want to tell my stories, get it all out before I'm off my rocker (or in it, as the case may be). Here are a few short hints for your climb up various ladders to success.

My first firm went broke in 1973 and was acquired for nothing by a new Wall Street company. I went along with the merger and reported for duty early one Monday in the fall. That first morning, I walked into my new personal office, a converted conference room, carrying my account books and a few pictures to hang on the wall. I was greeted by two men pummeling each other on the floor. One of them was the head institutional salesman, the other the man who ran the office support staff. The staff person had thrown out everything in the conference room to make way for me. This included the salesman's tax forms for the last five years.

The battlers were pulled apart. "Welcome to the firm," someone said to me, laughing about it. Later in the day, the biggest hitter in the office (the biggest producer of commissions) came along to sniff me out, thinking about competition for him. Like a dog sniffing a rival.

"So what's your deal?" he asked me.

"What do you mean, 'my deal'?" I said. "My company went broke."

"Let me give you some advice," the big hitter said to me. "If you ever have any clout in life, ask for things: salary raise, expense account, perks. If you don't have nonnegotiable demands when you're hot, fuhgeddaboudit when business turns bad. Every year you should ask for *something*, even if you don't need anything. If you're producing business, you're king, never forget it."

"I figured," I replied, "that if I do my job, I'll get rewarded."

He cocked a skeptical eye at me. "Don't be a jerk," he said. "You got a lot to learn."

The next day the head of our region called me from New York. "I'd like to take you to lunch next week," he

said. So we went to the Union Oyster House, the oldest restaurant in Boston, and sat in a small booth. The
regional head was a jolly big man with milk-white hair.
He loved the Red Sox and had come up from the sales
ranks into management.

"So," he said, smiling, "have a drink. How's things so
far at the new place?"

"Fine," I said, "but I'm going to need an expense
account." He continued to smile. "No problemo," he
said. I had paid attention to the big hitter. But I honestly
couldn't think of anything else to ask for, in my innocence. But I blurted out, "One thing more."

"Whatever we can do to make you happy."

Remember this, grandchildren, if anyone ever asks
you this. Have answers that reflect your sense of worth
while the romance is fresh.

"I want my office painted yellow," I said. I honestly
couldn't think of anything else.

The regional manager looked at me as if I were putting him on. "You're putting me on," he answered.

But I guess I was serious. He laughed, I'm sure,
relieved that what I wanted could be done on the cheap.
And also that I probably would be a pushover in the
future, and a little bit weird to boot. Our office manager
got his out-of-work brother-in-law to paint my office yellow over a weekend. It cost him two hundred dollars.

The big hitter was right about a key lesson: Don't

be shy about your value to the workplace. Be your own advocate.

Love,
Your formerly shy Papa

If you ever have clout in life, ask gently for more.

Cycles Are Eternal

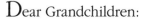

Dear Grandchildren:

"Real estate can never do anything but go up." I have heard that phrase many times in my life and it has always been proven wrong. I keep hammering away at this point all through my correspondence with both of you: no matter what the headlines, human nature never changes. Fear always replaces greed and vice versa. The good eventually replaces the bad. And vice versa.

Real estate in Southern California, for instance, has always been volatile. Since the 1970s, I have traveled to Los Angeles and stayed at the Hotel Bel-Air, my favorite in the United States. It's a romantic refuge on Stone Canyon Road that always reminds me of golden Hollywood days of the past. Over the years I'd go out in the mornings there and run a mile up the street, a mile back. Once a decade, nothing for sale, prices through the roof.

The next decade, FOR SALE signs every third house, places looking shabby, evidence of neglect and sadness, prices tumbling.

In the mid-1980s, your Mimi and I bought a house for investment, a seaside cottage in a new development that we thought we could rent to others. We already owned our beach house, several miles down the road from the cottage, the place you have visited all of your young lives. "This will be a great investment someday," I told your grandmother. "The world is not creating new beachfront property." This is an old cliché and it may have truth in it. But it has nothing to do with whether you make or lose money on the property. We rented it out for ten years, basically making back the annual costs, condo fees, and taxes. But renters, even nice people, tend to wreck a house. And we learned something about ourselves. Being a landlord was a giant pain in the neck. And we were bad at small pains in the neck. We sold the house at a $25,000 loss after ten years. "So much for real estate only going one way," I said.

"You'll make it up in the stock market," Mimi said. And I did. But the lesson about cycles sunk in. If I had waited another five years we would have tripled our money. Right about the property. Wrong about the timing. I concentrated here on real estate. But the lesson applies to all investments. Everything fluctuates. The nice thing about stocks is, unlike real estate or art, stocks are almost totally liquid. Win, lose, or draw, you can get out overnight. This is called liquidity. I believe that the more liquid one's assets, the better. And if your debt is nonexistent or manageable, it means you can buy more of your favorite stocks when the cycle is down. This has worked for your Papa in every down cycle in stocks that I've seen over fifty years in business. Cycles can be your friend. Play them to your advantage.

Your cyclical (but constant for you) grandfather

**Fear always replaces greed
and vice versa.**

Don't Be a Headline Reader

Wesley and Alyssa:

As you plot your financial futures, how to invest your own money or how to invest for others, if that's the profession you choose, here is some key advice: Do not be a headline reader. This means never being whipped into an emotional frenzy by what the media trumpets to us on a daily basis. To manage your own money you have to think over the chasm and try to predict the future. Do not dwell on last week or next week. The big money in life, whether it's in stocks or real estate, or stamps or coins or paintings, is made long term. Yes, we are talk-ing *years*.

I write this letter to you in a time of high anxiety. I know I've mentioned this before, but I want to under-score it. We are almost into the fourth year of the greatest economic upheaval around the world since the global depression of the 1930s. You will still feel it and hear it from your friends as you graduate from school. I know you're already hearing it and probably nervous about what's waiting for you out there. Here's a thought I'll bet no one has ever shared with you: every day for the rest of your lives, the news is going to be terrible! The media, including blogs and tweets, surrounds us and keeps the level of anxiety high. But if you're in business, engaged in life, you are *not* curled up in a ball saying, "The sky is falling." You are out there trying to beat the competition, rebranding yourself, doing what you have to do to put food on the table and go out and thrive. You have to screen out the terrible news and make your way. The daily events of the world will mostly have nothing to do with you and your careers. And people will tell you, because of *their* reactions to the news, "Now's not a time to start a business," "It's a horrible time to become a doctor," "America doesn't manufacture anything anymore," "Who would run for office these days, they'll rip you apart." Don't pay any attention to negative energy. Whatever your dream is, go for it.

Your Papa, who is a headline *scanner,* but a
believer in reading between the lines

Always have a dream.

The Value of Travel

Grandchildren:

There is a danger in never getting out and seeing the world. You have your heads down, making the donuts, or whatever you do, and thinking that wherever you are is the center of the universe.

This is not true, of course, and you now know it from experience. Alyssa and Wesley, your sailing adventure last summer on the Baltic, a working journey, was priceless. I know that if you looked in the mirror and were honest with yourselves, you'd say, "Not much studying, I'm afraid." That's fine. I actually believe that the true education in college is received from your fellow classmates and friends from ten o'clock at night until three in the morning. It's all about people from almost every corner of the world shootin' the breeze. My freshman year in college I was surrounded by such characters as a friend who went to high school at Le Rosey in Switzerland, where royalty went. He wore ascots around his neck and was the first husband of the movie star Ali MacGraw, of *Love Story* fame. He painted such images of romance to me, his school moving into the mountains for winter term and into the lush valleys for spring and fall. He put wanderlust into my dreams, the itch for travel.

One of your Papa's half-baked ideas is the concept of "having your eyes out on sticks." This means always being filled with curiosity, about people and places. And taking almost nothing at face value. So travel becomes a "magical mystery tour," as the Beatles would say. All of this eventually can be very valuable for investing, whether for clients or yourselves. For instance, if I had never strayed from Boston, it would have been years before I heard of companies that became wildly popular in other parts of America, before they came public: Starbucks and Nordstrom in the Pacific Northwest; Home Depot in Atlanta, Ryanair in Ireland, WPP advertising in London, Novartis in Switzerland, all successful companies that I discovered in my travels or were introduced to me by clients in far-off places.

Several years ago in Vienna I had what I call a "boing" moment, when suddenly a concept occurs to me, or a creative idea I'd never thought before. I had never been in Vienna. Your Mimi and I were wandering the streets on a fine fall Saturday. Thousands of people were wandering as well, pushing strollers, shopping, taking the air, holding their faces up to the sun. "Look around," I said to your grandmother. "Thousands of people enjoying a day off, spending money, being with their families. The terrorists, the nihilists, will never ultimately win. Because the vast majority of people in this world want only one thing: peace and the good life for themselves and their families. One *has* to be optimistic about the possibilities to make a business thrive, with the whole world becoming potential customers. Virtually every person you are seeing in Vienna today wants *things*, consumer goods. If you and I own the great companies that sell to the world, we will prosper."

"Let's start now," Mimi said. "See that storefront with windows up three stories? We'll start at the top and work our way down."

"And tonight, the opera."

"Mozart," she said. And it was.

Get out there, grandchildren. And keep your eyes out on sticks when you travel. It can be expensive, but if you view your wanderings as new ways to look at the world, ways that can expand your understandings of global businesses, the expense can be turned into personal capital gains.

Love,
Your Papa, whose eyes are always out on sticks

Keep your eyes out on sticks.

The Importance of Being Well Dressed

❧

Grandchildren:

I can't resist saying a few words here on dressing up/dressing down. There is a large advertising agency in my office building. They employ almost five hundred people, and I ride the elevator every day with many of them. They all seem to me to be twenty-seven years old and they look like they live on the streets like the squee-gee people who used to descend on drivers at traffic lights in Manhattan.

Grandchildren, part of the unfairness of life is that we're always being tested and evaluated, no matter how old we are. I have friends in their late sixties who have bought winter houses in Florida or California and wanted to join certain clubs. Someone from the husband's past, and it can be from grammar school, remembers a slight from years ago and won't let them in. As I told you, we're always being tested. So, particularly in a strange new setting, make sure that people viewing you for the first time don't pigeonhole you, don't put you in any box that might say, "Those kids look like they were brought up in a barn."

Here are a few basic lessons in dressing for almost any occasion, for interviews, for social events. For you, Wesley, it's really simple. Always have a blue blazer, two of them: one in wool for winter, lightweight for summer. The same for pants; grey flannel in winter, lighter weight the rest of the year. A good leather belt, dark socks, two pair of good leather shoes or loafers, one pair black, one brown.

Think this is boring? Mimi and I once went to Jack Nicholson's house in Los Angeles. It was the year he won the Academy Award for *One Flew over the Cuckoo's Nest*. He was wearing a white linen suit, no tie, and white patent leather shoes, no socks. It looked to us as if he didn't spend a minute thinking about the outfit. But now I'll bet he thought about everything, all the details, and how he'd look to others. So you darlings are probably not going to be Jack Nicholson or Katharine Hepburn (the first woman to be allowed to wear slacks in the old Ritz-Carlton in Boston). But you both can be distinctive in small, colorful ways.

Wesley, have your dress shirts dry cleaned, not washed by yourself or others. These have to look crisp.

Two ties for the rest of your life, one a rep (striped) in bold colors, and one with a pattern. Also, have two black turtleneck sweaters, one cotton, one wool. Any man will look fine in these underneath those blazers. Armed with these basics, you can appear anywhere in the world and look just perfect for any business or social challenge. You don't need red high-tops like your Papa; *want* is a lot different than *need*.

Alyssa: These are tips from your Mimi, who was a natural in all matters of dress. She just "got it," the way an actress like Audrey Hepburn was a natural. And a lady in the true sense of the word. Mimi has said, "Obviously, the little black dress; perfect anywhere. And one really good purse; you cannot have what looks to be an expensive suit or dress coupled with a cheap-looking purse. Scrimp and save to have one really good suit, a classic that will look fine for years.

"Walk all over Paris," Mimi has said. "The women in that city, from shop girls to queens of society, have a 'look' that implies being adventuresome with your dress: scarves worn many ways. Carry yourself as if you have secret passions. Even if, at the moment, you don't." Mimi added other tips for you over the years, but I'm going to underscore them now. "Try not to overload your wardrobe with current department store fads. The orange cashmere sweater is probably a total loss item, even if you bought it on the third markdown. The staples of your wardrobe should dictate your own style. They should include as many pieces of fine quality, bought slowly, as you can afford. Don't be afraid to mix in a Chanel suit with a T-shirt underneath from the Gap. Classics last, and they are timeless."

"Then what should every woman have?" I asked.

"I'd have that great Chanel suit and/or the same in a St. John knit. One fabulous black blazer, a few really good cashmere sweaters, one pair of fine pants in black, gray, and white, and one wonderful shawl and a knock-out pair of dressy boots. Again, hunt the stores for sales and accumulate these classics over time."

"Anything else?" I asked.

"Never marry anyone prettier than you."

Mimi is my last word on taste and style. As I've said, a natural.

But remember, you two, she loves you whatever you wear.

Papa

Think about how you present yourself.

Losing a Job

Dear Grandchildren:

This is an extension of one of my eternal lessons: all life is relationships. I've hammered at this in previous letters. But an incident at work this week made me think that my value to you guys extends to the "what ifs" and the "oh, my gods."

In this economic firestorm of the last several years, millions of Americans have been downsized, terminated, let go, offered a package—fired. Yesterday, Jean, a woman who has worked here for fourteen years, was told after lunch that her job had been eliminated. That's it. And as she was escorted to the elevators, she was told that any belongings would be shipped to her. Civility in the workplace, along with standards in society, seem to your old Papa at an all-time low.

I realize that every generation says the same things.

It comes with the aging process and the realization that we may be losing our relevance, that time is passing us by, and that today's technology revolutions are making us feel inadequate and, yup, just plain old. But as you take your hankies out of your pockets, know that I'm not just saying all this out of outrage. I'm trying to point out a law of business life: be prepared for the unexpected.

Andy Grove, the founder of the great company Intel, said, "Only the paranoid survive." I have this quotation pinned to my office door. Planning for clients' financial lives, I tell them, "Let's figure *worst* case scenario in our future, not *best* case." Usually, worst case never happens. But I want clients to get to the peace of mind stage and, I've found, figuring in the potentials, good *and* bad, gives clients a sense that we've really thought about all the issues during our sessions.

So how do we factor in the potential for losing our jobs? Can we ever plan for this? Well, back to relationships. I have a very smart client and friend who told me, "If I ever get fired, I have had a list for years, which I upgrade, of the first five people I would call to get me back on track, who would help me network or even offer me a new job."

This friend, a woman high up in her company and industry, was indeed let go herself, in a complete surprise when new management (mostly a bad thing in my experience) decided to put in their own team. These are the realities of often cold, cruel corporate life. And you two should be prepared to cover your own flanks—and your backs. A small degree of paranoia can be good. It can mean you're considering all the different possibilities in the increasingly difficult American workplace.

My woman friend hit the decks running, had a new résumé in her hand (she rewrites hers yearly to freshen it up). She contacted her list of smart people immediately. They hugged her to their bosoms, started spreading their nets, and my friend had a new job, in a new field, within three months, at essentially what she was making before. I contrast this with a story of another client, a man in Chicago, high up the food chain in a creative field. He was caught totally unprepared for his bad news. He won't return phone calls, stays in bed for days on end. He cannot dig himself out of depression and finds it impossible to cope with his feelings that "it's over."

My next few letters will be about how you both can help ensure you keep and build your own circle of people who can help make your career days more productive and smart. These will be your "smart people" letters.

Love from your serious Papa

A small degree of paranoia can be good.

Work in a City

Grandchildren:

I've told you this many times, but for years I've counseled young people like yourselves, probably several dozen a year. They want to write, or they want to come into the money business. Most of all they're concerned, sometimes frightened about where they fit in, getting a job, what's out there.

Just this week, a young man came to my office, referred by his family, who are my clients. Jay was well mannered, well groomed, curious, smart, and worried. "I'm in the retail business," he told me, "a junior financial officer, working on the books. The store is a part of a national chain. But it's in a rundown part of town, in a place where unemployment is high, people are depressed. I commute almost an hour each way, every day. I've got to get out. I've applied for a new job in banking, entry level. The job is closer to where I live with my folks. But it's another depressed community, slammed by loss of manufacturing jobs. Pay is okay, but I'm scared of being lost. I know no one in that town."

"Stop," I told him. "You're in your early twenties, just starting your business life. Do *not* take the bank job. Think about it. I tell everyone, and I'll keep repeating it, that all life is relationships. All of us, particularly when we're young, need life around us. Take almost any entry level job in an industry or business you're curious about. But it must be in a city. You must have life and people around you. In a city environment you will meet others, gain friendships, build a network, partially through your social life as well. It is these new associations that will get you better jobs, start kicking you up the ladder. Be gregarious, pursue hobbies. Work in a city when you start in the big world."

That's what I told the young man, and his brightened smile made my day. I think it's the right advice for you two as well. We can always retire to the country.

Love,
Your urban Papa

You have to have life around you.

Bonds Are Boring

Wesley and Alyssa:

Yup, bonds are boring, but they can be useful, if you can learn the basics of them early in your careers, because bonds can be part of your eventual investment options.

Stripping all this to plain vanilla, bonds are evidence of debt. Say that Kraft Foods wants to borrow some money. They issue bonds to raise this money. These bonds may pay you 5 percent a year interest, and will mature (or come due) in ten years. You believe in the solidity of Kraft's business (mac 'n' cheese, among other things), and you like the 5 percent the bonds pay you. Bonds are an obligation of the corporation issuing them. They must return your money when the bonds mature and pay you interest during the life of the bond. Simple, right?

But you can never get rich on these bonds. You hope they return all your money you've loaned them and pay you during the life of that obligation. I was brought up being taught that bonds were the conservative route to investing and you could only really prosper with them if you never spent the interest but let it compound. Eight percent interest doubles your money in nine years. These days, most people would jump at that. If you've read this far, Papa's keeping you from way more interesting things. But stay with it and tuck it away for future use. I suppose I'm looking for immortality, wanting you to save my letters.

During the 1970s, a period of high inflation, you could buy U.S. Treasury bonds paying 15 percent. You could buy tax-free bonds issued by cities, states, and towns paying as much as 10 percent. Tax free. If I could get these rates today, who needs the stock market? During this period, I had a client who offered me a bribe if I could supply someone willing to be a courier, who would carry several million dollars' worth of bonds in a bag with a hidden compartment to St. Maarten to stick in a safe deposit box for him. He had bought them with cash he had skimmed (as his son, years later, revealed to me) from an outlet factory store he owned. He wanted to hide these assets from his wife and provide an eventual getaway stash for himself. I fired him as a client and years later heard that he had given most of his money to the con man Bernie Madoff. A clear example of "what goes around, comes around."

Basically, bonds, as I said, are universally viewed as conservative, stocks as risky. But basic bonds are no protection against inflation, which can destroy the value of your money over time. Inflation can be a killer. For instance, the 1913 dollar today is worth only a nickel. The 1945 dollar is worth nine cents. The 1980 dollar is worth 50 cents. Over the years stocks have given real inflation protection. No contest versus bonds, which provide none of this protection.

This is a bare bones, simple introduction to "the other side of the balance sheet," which is debt. At your ages, when you start to invest money of your own, buy stocks for growth, and perhaps for some dividend income as well. But long-term growth of your money is what you both should be interested in for at least the next twenty-five years. I don't believe in any formula approach to money. There's an old investment cliché, "Own your age in bonds, the rest in stocks." This would mean at age thirty, put 30 percent in bonds and 70 percent in stocks. I tend to ignore all investment clichés except two: The first is "Buy low, sell high." And the other is trust in the resilience of the American spirit to eventually turn things around. I don't think I'm a fool. But I am a long-term optimist.

Let's just strip the rhetoric away and simplify it.

Now's the time for you to take chances in life, for experiment and risk. Bonds for income, stocks for growth. Go with stocks. Investing for yourselves will teach you a lot about how *you* perceive value and how those perceptions get bounced around by market movements. If you pay attention, it will teach you a lot about your tolerance for risk. Good lessons for both of you.

Love,
From your still occasionally aggressive Papa

**Now's the time for taking
chances in life.**

There Are People You Cannot Save from Themselves

Wesley and Alyssa:

You can never tell about the gene pool. In my opinion, it dictates almost everything. That said, who knows the reasons for both of you seeming to be responsible people who care for others. This is a wonderful characteristic and, no matter how often I can complain about this in myself, I would much rather be the one with strong shoulders than to be the needy one.

So I want to warn you about this need or ability to care for people who lean on you both. *There are people you cannot save from themselves.*

What do I mean by this? As I pour out my (sometimes half-baked) life lessons to you, I want to include areas you haven't thought about yet in your young lives. I mean particularly areas that can suck the oxygen out of a room, that sap your energy in ultimately useless and futile ways.

I had a friend years ago who had two marriages by the time he was fifty. In each case, he would ask multiple people, "I think she's the girl for me. Is she the girl for me?" Virtually everyone asked, in each case, said, "We don't think so."

"Well," he'd answer, "maybe you're right." But he married them anyway. Both marriages ended in divorce, but not without years of phone calls, breakfasts, lunches, dinners with him replaying the old movies. Then there were his business ventures, with him always asking friends for money to get things started. All of the ventures were "sure things," "bound to hit it big." Every one of them failed over the years. My friend was funny, charming, well educated. And needy. He was relentless in his calls and visits, always insisting that "this time is different."

So I've learned the hard way that there are people like this, bound to us in friendship, sometimes from childhood, who take and take, particularly of your time.

In many ways this situation is like owning a stock you thought was a good idea to buy. And you buy some at $50, knowing it will be a winner for you. But, for various reasons, the stock starts to go down. You stay with it, feeling it cannot go below $45. Then at $40, you can't believe what a bargain it is. Finally at $20, having ridden it all the way down, you can't stand looking at it anymore and sell the stock. You have to take your losses in friendships as well, as sad and somewhat cruel as this sounds. But knowing the downside about relationships that sap your energy *and* your pocketbook can be beneficial to your mental health.

Know your characters.

Your loving Papa, who will never be a
burden to you (that's a joke)

Beware of the takers.

Have Long-Term Friends of the Opposite Sex

Grandchildren:

Men are no longer from Mars and women just from Venus. These days, we're all from everywhere. When your Mimi and I were married, the roles for men and women were clearly defined. No matter where in America you lived, the man was the breadwinner and went to a job every day. The woman kept the house and raised the children.

Today, it's difficult to even define relationships. A sardonic friend called recently and said, "You wanna marry a goat? And if you're in love, who says a goat won't make a great spouse? The sky's the limit these days." Well, if the sky's the limit, it's more important than ever to have friends of the opposite sex. And I mean pristine friendships, no sex involved. There, grandchildren, I actually said the word I haven't mentioned in my letters to you—sex. Now it's out of the way. My parents had two kids, me and my younger sister. I remember her saying to me when she was about fourteen, "Yuck. How could you ever think about Mom and Dad 'doing it'? What a turnoff. Bad enough they did it twice, right?" You probably would not be surprised at how many young people think and have said the same thing.

I believe that if you are ever going to manage people or run a business, you'd better have a friend of the opposite sex with whom you can have free, frank, and often funny conversations. Here are just a few examples of what I've learned from my female buddies, ladies both older and younger than me.

My oldest woman friend is in her eighties. She doesn't hide her age. She tells me, "All I'm looking for is a dirty old man with a clean body." She sends me presents occasionally, like notepads with my photo on them and the quotation "Whatever it is . . . no." She loves giving presents, and I've tried to layer some restraint over her generosity to others, including me. "I was in retail sales until I was in my seventies," she always reminded me. "And I'd throw in a little extra to every customer I waited on: a perfume sample, a conditioner, a blush. And I'd give them restaurant, movie tips, as well. 'Sylvia's Services,' I'd tell them. And it separated me from the crowd of other salespeople. Be a little different if you sell *any-thing*," she said. And I've always remembered that.

On the "different" angle, I've had a woman lawyer

friend who told me when we met, "I don't want to have anyone forget me. So I'll tell you a little story. I wanted my husband to have a special fortieth birthday present. He's a big Democrat. So I took a trip to Providence, Rhode Island, went to a tattoo parlor. And had a donkey tattooed on my left butt."

"Let's see it," I said.

"Well," she answered, "I won't show it to you, but I did get up on the firm's copy machine and—here." She whipped out a copy of her tattoo and said, "What a tribute to a husband. You can imagine how much thought and creativity I'd put into *your* legal problems."

Every time someone came to me after that, looking for a street-smart lawyer, I referred them to her. Sadly, for me, she became a judge and stopped taking private clients. But she had told me a few precious principles of hers, like:

1. Unless you're a nuclear physicist, you need human interaction. And remember, in that interaction the most important quality is a sense of humor. Because people are really terrified of one another.
2. We are not practical people; we believe what we see on the screen. I have handled hundreds of divorce cases and I know that marriage is something you have to work at every day, like constantly negotiating a peace treaty. American men won't believe that you cannot just marry for love.

3. Never overlook the obvious when dealing with people on any level. Tip O'Neill, the former Speaker of the House, once asked a woman in his district if she voted for him. "No," the woman said to the long-time congressman.

"Why not?" asked the surprised O'Neill.

"You never asked," the woman answered.

4. If you can tell a joke, you'll always sell more tomatoes than anyone else.

Another woman, whom I called "the Countess," had been an actress on Broadway and starred in silent films. She was a client, the mother of good college friends, and had ended up, after her acting career, as the first head of the U.S. Committee to UNICEF. She told me, "Here's an eternal truth that will help you in understanding some of the truths about women. These truths can help you in business and in marriage, *if* you ever marry. If you don't, it will steer you in difficult times in your relationships. I've seen tough times," she said. "The Depression, World War II when my husband was killed. I know that when times are tough, we revert to our basic essentials from millions of years ago. It is woman's nature to be the caretaker, caregiver, nurturer to the family. She is the mother wolf; the true protector of home and hearth. And she will do this in the work environment as well. It's bred into us." She smiled. "Man's basic nature is to go out, kill the brontosaurus, and bring home the steaks. Remember the basics in human nature and screen out what seems to be popular at the moment."

As an author, my friendships with women have, I think, made me better able to craft them as characters in realistic ways. As a businessman, I hope I'm sensitive to the opposite sex as well and try to appreciate them. It can help your business function more efficiently and profitably.

I have lots of quickie phrases and comments of wisdom from my women friends and clients that I come back to often. One woman advertising executive told me right before I married your Mimi, "When you two start a family and pressures build in the office, it is key to remember, 'Don't be a pain in the butt around the house.'" This has been good advice for more than forty years.

Alyssa, I'll have a letter all for you, with street smart advice from men to women. I'm taking notes on it as you read this. Nope, you're not chopped liver, I'm just trying to make the milk and the chocolate cake finish at the same time.

Your loving Papa

When times are tough, we revert to our basic essentials.

Negotiations

Grandchildren:

A rather quick note this week (a relief, I'm sure). And this lesson may surprise you, the way it really surprised me years ago.

I once was in a deal to open an Italian restaurant with several partners. My job was to raise the money.•
Paul, my consultant partner, was to be the person to oversee real estate leases and be chief financial officer, watching all purchases, dealing with accountants and lawyers. The last two partners were the creatives—two brilliant and famous chefs with shows on public television. We hired a food consultant at one point to advise us on packaging our own sauces and pasta. The bills seemed very large to us. When I talked to Paul about it, he said, "Don't even think about it. The bill's five thou-

sand dollars. We're offering twenty-five hundred, and maybe, maybe we go to three k."

"But," I said, "I always thought a bill was a bill, and you have to pay it."

"I have news for you," Paul said. "A bill is just the *beginning* of the negotiations."

By golly (that's what grandparents say), the consultant agreed to cut his bill to $2,900. "All in life is negotiable," Paul said to me, "and the earlier in your life you understand this, the more money you'll save. But you have to be tough-minded about the process. It's a technique not designed to make you friends."

I've used this a lot over the years, despite being insecure enough to want to be liked. Mostly, I use it when buying art or jewelry for Mimi. It *always* works.

Your sometime parsimonious, papa

All life is negotiable.

Make Yourself Memorable

Grandchildren:

This is a letter about something that happened to me today and a practical lesson for you both. Three years ago a young man called on me in my office. He was born in Korea and had just graduated from college in America. His name is Bom Kim. He came to me looking to entice me to invest some money in an entrepreneurial venture of his, a new magazine. He billed it as the *Vanity Fair* for his particular famous college, full of (in his view) rich, sophisticated, literate graduates who would pay up for smartly written tales by and about these graduates and their adventures in life.

I was taken by his enthusiasm and his game plan. He told me what the minimum investment in the magazine was. I told him, "I'm interested in a taste, not full price.

And I think I can help you in creative ways with the project."

"Like, what were you thinking?" he asked.

"I was thinking about a third of your figure."

"No one else has suggested this," he said.

"Well," I said, "I admire you. And I believe in betting on people, not concepts. I'm willing to bet you can make this work. But I'm also only willing to put up the figure I mentioned."

"Let me think about it," he said. We shook hands and he left. Two days later, he called and said, "Unconventional. But I've learned to expect this in America. You're in."

Seven months later, Bom Kim called me and said, "I'm happy to tell you that the magazine is being sold— for double the money you put in."

Believe me, kids, this is the first time this ever happened to me in my life. And in a later letter, I'll deal with private, illiquid investments and the pitfalls that can occur with them. But this time it was a great experience. The real lesson in this comes later. Bom Kim kept in touch, e-mailing every six months or so to tell me what he was doing. A year or so ago, he said he was enrolling in business school. I wished him well, grateful to be kept in the loop by someone who had doubled my investment in a short time. Two days ago, Bom Kim called and asked if he could come to see me. In he came today, looking more mature, more confident. "I'm getting married this summer," he told me. "A classmate in college; Chinese from Taiwan. She's a lawyer, going to work in San Francisco."

"That's wonderful," I told him. Bom Kim went on. "I just wanted to stop by in person and thank you for being my supporter in the past. It meant a lot to me, and it always will." He took my hand in both of his and shook it firmly, smiling at me while he did it. "I'm off to Korea tomorrow to start a new venture. Dropped out of business school to do it. The experience was fine. But life is far more interesting than school."

So, several interesting observations. I'd do almost anything for young Mr. Kim, because he never forgets a kindness and he burns no bridges. He stays in touch with his past and builds his Rolodex of people who would help him in the future. And he, a master of technology and all things digital, understands the importance of the personal touch. Wisdom comes from all ages, and it pays attention to the little things.

Your always willing to be surprised grandfather

Burn no bridges.

Private Investments

Grandchildren:

Time to discuss private or alternative investing. This is also *illiquid* investing, since, once in, it is often time-consuming and difficult to get your money out. Private investments can be incredibly lucrative. Imagine that someone influenced you to invest in Apple, or Google, or Microsoft *before* they came onto the public market. You could have made hundreds of times your money, sometimes thousands of times; riches beyond compare. Mostly, however, these dreams turn to dust.

America is an entrepreneurial nation. We like to invent things, we like to start companies, many of us like to work for ourselves and not for others. We believe the sky's the limit for us.

You both will face lots of investment decisions over the range of your lives. Some of these decisions will involve areas where you may not be able to sell when you want to. Most of these private investments are in so-called limited partnerships. This means that there are general partners who put a deal together, do the legal work, raise the money from you, the limited partners. Limited means that your potential loss is limited to the amount you put up. No one can sue you for more, no matter how bad the deal turns out.

Here's the exciting part, a peek at some of the deals I've put money into over the years. Most of them, I should say, I did for educational purposes, not to get rich. Among many other things my dad hammered into me were his words, "No one else is going to make you rich; you're going to have to do it yourself. And remember, most of life is really hard, punctuated by moments of brilliance."

So far, his advice has been correct. And because I always put relatively small amounts into these deals, if they completely blew up, it didn't change our lives. Private equity companies *used* to say, "Your money's tied up for five to ten years, but you can make ten times, twenty times *more* on your money." Fine. I'll believe it when I see it.

Aside from not committing bank-breaking amounts to prospective deals, I always believed in betting on the person and not the concept. Here are some of the diverse private deals in which your somewhat weird

Papa has invested. My first enterprise was a travel and study abroad company, geared to high school students. I was given stock in this company and helped raise the funds to start it. So, none of my cash in, just what they call "sweat equity." I'd work by giving advice and doing some networking in exchange for a piece of the action. In the stock market at the time, one of the biggest fads was the youth market; young people with plenty of money to spend. Any company that was targeting this demographic became a hot stock.

Raising money for my company was easy; people wanted to cash in on the new rage. The first year, everyone, including me, got a big dividend that almost gave us back a quarter of our investments. But another year later, the youth fad crashed, along with our private company. Recession kicked in. Good people, good management. But young people and their parents increasingly could not afford travel abroad.

As time went on, I invested in two partnerships our firm had put together as perks for supposedly their top people. It was a commitment for about ten years. Both of them recently closed down. In ten years, I got back a little more than I had put in. Barely. The same amount of money invested into money market funds would have given me more, and I could have gotten out any day. Liquidity means the ability to sell immediately, win, lose, or draw.

Are you getting the picture?

Various other bets of mine have included a movie production company, a trotter horse, a computer software company, an Italian restaurant, a beach house for rental purposes, an educational consulting firm, a wine importing company specializing in Italian vineyards, a TV commercial producer, and a magazine (about which I've written to you earlier).

These investments were part of my graduate school education, but much more valuable, I think, than business school because theoretical investing does not involve emotion. I had lots of emotion about my money in these projects. But, if I was excited or angry, I couldn't get out of them until they went public, sold out—or crashed and burned, giving me a capital loss for my tax returns. I've retained the lessons from all these ventures. And I end up believing what my father told me: "No one is going to make you rich except you." Fifty years in business has reinforced that notion. Never bet the ranch on someone else's dream.

Your private Papa

**No one's going to make you rich
except you.**

Do Your Due Diligence

Grandchildren:

I'm old-fashioned. I believe in handshakes and looking people in the eye. "A man's word is his bond" was the concept I grew up with. But not everyone was raised this way, even years ago. And they certainly aren't raised this way today.

If you ever hire anyone for a job, it's fine to trust your instincts. But you'd better do a lot more before you let that contractor, plumber, doctor, lawyer, or money manager into your lives. I know there's Craigslist and endless sites to explore to check people out. But no source is foolproof, and not everyone is documented enough to prevent disappointment or disaster. Ronald Reagan supposedly said, "Trust, but verify." That's good advice.

So here are a couple of stories that were surprising to me, both pre-Internet. When Mimi and I moved into the city from the suburbs, we bought an old townhouse that had been gutted entirely and was to be completely renovated by the seller, using his own contractors. The seller's chief henchman did all the hiring and for various reasons fired all the initial craftspeople. One of the new guys, Lenny, seemed incredibly competent and eager to get the job done. He pointed out that much of the work that had been done was finished badly. He ripped it all out and began a beautiful restoration. At later stages I had to kick in a lot of our own money, and the bills kept coming.

"You guys treat me like gold," Lenny said. And he told us of his days as a sniper in Vietnam, and the work he had done on his own house: birdbaths, picket fences, a pool, a cupola, a garage that looked like a chalet. We were charmed by him and loved the work so far, loving also the tales and pictures of his family and children. Meanwhile, my checks flowed to him until one day, Lenny disappeared. So much work had been paid for but not done. After ten days, your Mimi was frantic. "We know his address, let's hunt him down." Off we went to the town where he lived, a former shoe and textile factory mecca, now gone into sad decline as those industries fled New England and moved to the South and, eventually, the Far East.

We drove into Lenny's neighborhood, a rundown,

decaying area, a remnant of the past. "Look for the white picket fence," your Mimi said. "And the beautiful, restored Victorian." All we saw was poverty and decay. We spotted the number Lenny had given us. It was a rooming house in disrepair—peeling paint, broken windows. I went up the stairs alone, looked at the multiple names on the mailbox. No Lenny. I knocked on the front door. Deserted. No cupola, no garage with vintage cars, no pool, no children. Nothing. My checks had been cashed, work left unfinished. We didn't even know if Lenny was his real name.

The bottom line? Don't trust a firm handshake and a look directly into your eyes. Do your homework on anyone who is anxious to work for you.

Some years ago I met a man at a club where I played squash. He would come there to work out, take a steam bath and shower, then have a beer in the locker room. He was also charming and seemed brilliant to me, quoting Einstein, Steinmetz (look him up), Mark Twain, Napoleon, endless philosophers and critics. He had helped to invent, he said, a business computer that would cut paperwork by two-thirds.

I introduced him to a man who would come into the squash locker room solely for a steam bath and a shower. He ran a school that supervised testing for public employees, like police and fire personnel. His name was Danaher, and he, too, was charmed by the work-out man. The charming man was divorced, and your Mimi fixed him up with a young woman she modeled with, a bouncy, sunny blonde. She lived with her grand-mother to save money and the dates with the charmer went well. Until one day, the grandmother called Mimi, frantic. "Where's Bonnie?" she screamed into the phone. "Bonnie hasn't come home in two days." It seemed the charmer had taken Bonnie to his house and locked her inside. She emerged safely after various arguments and told Mimi, "He's as loony as a Looney Tunes; mad as a hatter." I called Danaher to warn him. "I don't think you should buy that equipment; something about him is a little fishy."

"But he's so smart," Danaher said. "He even told me that his company stationery is buff and blue. That his research shows those colors are the easiest on the eyes. And he went to our college."

"The Unabomber went to our college," I answered. "You go to a wonderful school, it doesn't mean you're not nuts. Or dishonest."

Mr. Danaher lost his deposit. We had a beer one afternoon at the squash club. "He was so smart," he said to me. "So convincing."

These stories will not guarantee that you won't make mistakes about people. It's just a warning to both of you to be a bit cynical about people who are about to enter your life and promise you the moon, in various ways. It's sad even to write a letter like this to you, but innocence is tough to preserve these days. But your Papa will trust *your* word and handshakes *any* day.

Your grandfather

Trust, but verify.

What Hollywood Taught Me

Grandchildren:

When I went to college, many of my friends thought that, after graduation, they had to have a New York phase in their lives. I thought the same thing; after all, Frank Sinatra sang, "If I can make it there, I'll make it anywhere." But, it seems, for the last fifteen years, young people want to go west, to have a Hollywood phase in their lives.

Lessons abound in both of these experiences, but Los Angeles seemed to me to be an amazing American place for dreams. New York is exciting and depressing, smart and dumb as well, endlessly cocky, upscale and lowdown, as diverse a place as any on Earth. But when I think of Los Angeles, I only think of the movie business. It's seductive. And it's the only business I've ever been around where the people in it only talk about the business, the gossip, the scandals, the buzz. As I said, seductive. I was out there on and off for months in the 1970s, adapting a best-selling book, *The Money Game*, for the movies. My producer, David, a wild guy, raised Jewish in New Jersey, had converted to Subud, a religion founded in Indonesia. "Judaism is nowhere strong enough for me," he said. He was brilliant, I thought, and quirky. To pay my writer's fee, plus first class flights and hotels, he and his partner, unbeknownst to me, put all the charges on thirty credit cards, to each of which they would pay ten or twenty dollars a month to maintain. But I was seduced by all of the dreams of glory. I was going to be a *star*. Of course, it turned into nothing on screen, but was a wonderful respite from the financial world.

David used to take me up to Mulholland Drive and look over all of Los Angeles at night, millions of lights blinking up at us. "Look at this," David said, "the dream of every immigrant with a brain. We're gonna create the first movie about Wall Street to ever make money." Sounded good to me, and I was sucked into the program. David, the ambitious independent producer, in order to make some cash, delivered the *Wall Street Journal* before dawn to the residents of Bel Air. Flip, from his rolled down VW windows, to Tom Jones; flip to Dean Martin. All while coyotes howled and he was half asleep, for a hundred dollars a week. Anything to keep his dream alive.

David taught me how to write a script. He'd leave me to write in the mornings. Then he'd pick me up at noon, take me to lunch, and critique what I'd written. "Forget dialogue," he'd say. "You should be able to write an exciting movie all in action, not words. Words are for amateurs." Then we'd go to screenings at the Directors Guild in the afternoon, seeing several films that David wanted to emphasize to me: *American Graffiti* and *The Three Musketeers*, directed by Richard Lester, who had done Beatles movies. At dinner, David would tell me stories about Hollywood legends and screw-ups and inside stuff. Then he'd turn me loose to write for another two hours, having absorbed the lessons of the day. Every night he'd call me before I turned out my light.

"You promise you wrote for two hours?"

"Yup," I'd say.

"Remember," he'd sign off to me, "you gotta feel Gatsby's green light at the end of the dock; you gotta feel how it will all look when it gets dark in the theater and the magic rolls. Believe in the magic." Great training, grandchildren, for whatever you end up doing out there after school has faded.

Earlier in my life, fresh out of college, I went to L.A. Through friends' influence I had interviews at Paramount, Columbia, Twentieth Century–Fox, with heads of production, presidents, directors. In the office of one producer, who was clad in a giant yellow terry-cloth bathrobe at his desk, having just come out of his private shower, I was allowed to sit in on a story conference. Several writers were pitching a television series idea about two brothers in the American Civil War. The producer was leaning way back in his La-Z-Boy chair. His eyes were shut, hands folded over the tummy of his robe. In the middle of the writers' presentation, the producer jumped forward. "I see two helicopters," he said.

"You what?" one of the writers exclaimed. "This is the Civil War—1864."

"Look," said the producer. "I know what I see, and I see two helicopters. What can you do with it?"

When the writers left, the producer said to me, "You don't want to go through what it takes to make it in this town, kid. They're all liars and thieves and fools. Do yourself a favor. You've got a good education. Go into the family business. What do you need the aggravation for? You don't want to have to take showers in the middle of the day because everyone around you smells of fear. You can't wash off fear." He kept knotting and unknotting the belt of his robe. Not able to come up with a creative solution to two helicopters in the Civil War, I left his office.

No one in power wants to give you credit for being able to persevere. "You won't have the guts to do what I've done," they are saying. But they are also saying, "I don't want to be supplanted by the next generation. No one is going to push me out of the corner office or the chairmanship or my perks." So when, as a recent graduate, you interview for jobs, look around at the trappings of power: the private showers, the yellow terry-cloth robes, the oriental rugs on the floor. Look at what *you* can have if you're willing to bust your tail. Don't listen to discouraging words. They come from people who don't want competition or reminders that power changes hands.

The last show biz story I'll share with you two is about the brief time I was in Los Angeles promoting my book (don't laugh) *Sex and Money*. There was, in Hollywood language, "interest in the project." It came from two producer/writer brothers, famous for successful comedies. They had set up a lunch with Mel Brooks, the legendary funnyman, creator of *Young Frankenstein*, *Blazing Saddles*, *The Producers*, and so much more. We met at the Westwood Marquis, then a hot deal spot, great for gossip and people watching. As we all shook hands and sat down, Brooks wisecracking and crowing about a new movie about to come out, the shortest Beach Boy came to the table. "No matter what it is," he said, "how about we do the music?" Another man, teeth shining long before he reached us, stopped by and offered, "Any way there's a piece for me in this?" Brooks assured him, "Room for a lotta people, early in the game." When the schmoozing stopped for a minute, Mel Brooks looked at me, paused, and said, "Don't worry, kid, we'll take care of you." He told me later at lunch that he would be in Boston the following weekend for a bar mitzvah. "Stop by," he added. "It'll be at the Ritz."

Back home, I stopped by at the hotel to deliver a book in person to Mel Brooks. "Sorry," I was told, "no one by that name has registered."

Don't get me wrong, kids. I'm thrilled to have had these adventures. But all of them reasserted one of the most important business principles of my life: never spend the money people promise you until it's in your pockets.

And as an eternal lesson for any career you may pursue: You may often be surrounded by fools and incompetent superiors, but never lose sight of the many absurdities in life.

Your Papa, who still loves showbiz

Never spend the money until it's in your pocket.

Almost Nothing Happens the Way You Plan It

Wesley and Alyssa:

I could almost close this letter with the heading alone. So, lucky for you, this note is short this week, with just one thought to chew on.

I planned to be a full-time writer, a novelist who would never write nonfiction. Maybe I was uncomfortable with facts and only wanted to make things up. To support my writing dream, I planned to go into the advertising business, on the creative side, making up slogans for gadgets, writing jingles for soap. If someone told me at age twenty-two, "You'll be managing people's money for a living for more than *fifty* years," I'd tell them they were smoking something.

A client of mine, long dead, grew up in the Great Depression. He became a lawyer, specializing in political campaigns and the pursuit of power. I do love to hear stories of the past and try to relate them to the present. He told me, "I got out of law school in 1933, and if someone offered me a contract then for ten thousand dollars a year for life, I would've signed it in blood." Of course, he made many multiples of that figure eventually. When I got out of college, starting lawyers were paid $6,000. And that $10,000 figure annually, I *never* thought I'd achieve it. When Mimi and I bought our first house, we paid $62,000 for it, with more than three acres of land and a babbling brook running alongside the front yard. My father said at the time, "Whoever heard of paying sixty-two thousand dollars for a house? This will be Spooner's Folly." After seventeen years, we sold it for almost $400,000 and moved into the city.

One of my college roommates majored in government and was set on a career as an attorney. In our senior year, during Christmas break, he met an elderly pediatrician at a family party. The doctor, after a few drinks, told my roommate so many stories of delivering and helping babies that he came back to college, switched majors, and took an extra year of premed courses. He eventually became one of the most famous researchers into childhood infectious diseases.

Whatever you plan for life will not turn out as you thought. But it might be even better. Cultivate a sense of flexibility, you'll be better prepared for when plans go wrong. Or for when they go wondrously, unexpectedly, well.

I suppose what I'm really saying is, try to anticipate both sides of your planning processes: the ups and the downs.

Love,
Your often practical Papa

Cultivate a sense of flexibility.

Dealing with Loss:
Scar Tissue

Dear Alyssa and Wesley:

My first editor when I was writing novels told me, "You know, you can never really be a great novelist until you've experienced grief. And loss."

"Well," I answered, "I would think that if I'm a writer, I can imagine all that stuff."

"You can't really imagine it," he said. This was long before my parents and my grandparents died. Long before I'd lost any friends to accident or illness.

My dad died on Christmas morning, a day after his birthday. It was sudden, a heart attack in the hospital, on top of an earlier, milder, incident. There was no bleaker day in my life, picking out a casket at a funeral home, everyone else in the family at our house opening Christmas presents. Your parents, young children then, were not told that day. And, after I returned home, I had to fake it, no one wanting to spoil the kids' excitement. For me, every Christmas is bittersweet: happy thoughts of family when everyone seemed young, cold and chilly memories of the day my dad died.

There are other kinds of losses as well: romantic, employment, financial. Many of these can seem cata-strophic at the time they happen to you. But you will shake off these moments, as difficult as it may be to realize it then. We are a nation obsessed with ourselves. We like to talk about "us." And if we don't have really close friends who will listen, and counsel us as well, we are willing to pay for these professional ears: psychia-trists, psychologists, counselors of all kinds. If you guys are lucky, you will have a very few people in your lives whose brains, common sense, and discretion will pro-vide these needed therapies as friends.

Remember this about friendship: you have to work at it, you have to stay in touch. It won't automatically be there for you. Your parents, our own kids, have had a saying about people dear to them from the time *they* were kids. "It goes deep," they say. And the best friends do go deep.

We never really believe in death or loss when we're young; it's a faraway concept. I've always dealt with the tough stuff by searching for answers, solace in things much bigger than all of us. For reasons that I only partly understand, I need to be alone, to think through what all the tough things mean. I seek out the ocean and the beach, kicking the water as I walk along its edge. That's my therapy, mind wandering through the past and making various bargains and promises to myself about the future. This process involves following Peter Pan's advice—"Think lovely thoughts"—about people gone from my life, goals I didn't achieve, and determination to get 'em next time. That's part of both my mourning and my healing process.

You know all too well that your Mimi has been undergoing treatment for lung cancer for the last year and a half. Your grandparents may seem to you to be very social, always at parties, traveling with friends, having lunches and dinners with different people from distant places. The truth is, we're very private people, sometimes I even think somewhat selfish. We never really lived solely for our children and grandchildren, preferring to pick our spots in that regard, especially on weekends where we'd really retreat into filling up the cup again of privacy, catching up from busy weeks, preparing for the next busy week.

The last piece of advice in this letter is to always exercise physically and recognize its importance in getting through the rocky road adventures you'll experience. Both of you are athletes, used to the rhythm of sports and the energies your workouts give you. It has to be a lifetime pursuit, not something you abandon because your lives are too busy. I've found that if you're energized, you can handle almost anything. Sorry to rain on your young ways of thinking, which may include "we're immortal, in our twenties with everything ahead of us on the yellow brick road." I see my job as your grandfather to throw practical thoughts that go beyond next week or next year to you. I'm a cynic. Who else is going to do this?

Love from your sometimes somber Papa

Remember what goes deep.

Stay in Touch with Your Past

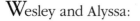

Wesley and Alyssa:

I wrote a book in 1979 called *Smart People*. Its major theme is that we lived in an increasingly anonymous world, where doctors never made house calls, plumbers never showed up on time, and there was an increasing perception that you could not get people to pay attention to you. These days those perceptions have gone through the roof. I know I've harped on the theme that relationships are everything. It's true, and it's one of the key lessons in life for you to know and to pass on to your own kids, if you're lucky enough to have them someday.

There are three key principles to building your team of smart people. The first is stay in touch with your past. Social networks are all the rage now. Both of you are on Facebook. Both of you tweet from time to time. These social media may sputter and die and be replaced by the next hot ideas. But it's the pull of the past that is the eternal lesson here, and the past will continue to resonate with both of you as you build your team of experts.

Few of us can resist the chance to reminisce with someone who shared a part of our childhood. Most of us are suckers for nostalgia, retaining memories of what has been when times were simpler and we were smaller. Try to maintain friendships from the past. And do what can be more important: keep high school yearbooks, Sunday school pictures, college yearbooks, club or fraternity directories, or refer to these organizations' sites on the Web. Never disdain school reunions. At these events you'll find key smart people who will simplify your life, and who cannot resist helping you because they all shared past experiences with you. People are pulled by these times.

Respond to high school alumni questionnaires. Respond to college reunion questionnaires. People I once considered cool would never consider replying to these inquiries. They would never consider looking back to look or be looked over. But those people are fools, in my view. There is no bond as strong as the past. And it becomes more important as you grow older.

When I moved to a new town when Mimi and I were first married, I consulted both my high school and college directories. Sure enough, Jack Ritter lived in the town, and Jack Ritter had made all of my manual-training class projects in seventh and eighth grade—the birdhouse, the lap desk, even the envelope holder in the shape of a cranberry picker. Jackie was now the town plumber, and, although we hadn't seen each other in years, he dropped several projects to fix pipes, redo bathrooms, and check heating systems for me when I called him.

What did I say to him? "Is this Jack Ritter, maker of the best birdhouses in the Baker School seventh grade?"

"Who is this?"

"Is this the Jack Ritter who couldn't go to his left for ground balls in the hole at shortstop?"

"Who *is* this?"

"Is this the Jack Ritter who saved my tail in grammar school and who is going to save me again when my bathroom drain clogs? This is John Spooner, Jack, how you doin'?"

"John Spooner," he said. "God, didn't you ever learn how to fix *anything*?"

Reminded of his past triumphs, he couldn't wait to save me again. And save us he did, many times in our new town.

But remember, you must call your Jackie Ritter *before* your bathroom drain clogs, *before* your pipe bursts, *before* your hot water heater explodes. You have to set up your team in advance of emergencies, not after they occur.

I jumped to the head of the line with Jack Ritter in

ten minutes of memories. Every time I see him, a few old stories ensure that I stay on the top of the list. And this must be a two-way street. I've helped him as well, with retirement planning and saving for his kids' education. This is not a cynical process. It should be done with affection.

And it doesn't matter if the people from the past were old enemies. Old school enemies can, in fact, work particularly well for you. At my twentieth grammar school reunion, I spotted Enid the Amazon. And she was gorgeous. Kids had given her the name "Enid the Amazon" in the third grade when she towered over all the boys. She hated me. I embraced her at the reunion, and she rushed over to her husband.

"You traumatized Enid's youth," he said to me. "She's told me thousands of times about her nickname and how she'd like to get back at you." We were adult now. Childish antagonisms were childish. We both laughed about it. I told her how terrific she looked and how wonderful it was for a woman to be tall. Enid and her husband ran one of the largest ticket agencies in New York. Whenever I needed impossible-to-obtain seats, Enid the Amazon came through for me. She had remembered me as making fun of her, but then at the reunion I honestly praised her. She could not refuse the human contact of someone from childhood, some strong association with friend or foe that reaffirms the past. Something we shared.

You have to make the effort to stay in touch. If you do, people will not resist. And they don't even have to be people you know well. I have called members of associations or clubs or classmates of mine in places like Watsonville, California; Memphis, Tennessee; and Panama City, Panama; and have been given the best of those towns. I have called these people and said, "Hi, I'm John Spooner. I grew up on your block years ago. I lived next to the Hathaways. Remember, they were the ones who put the cat in the washing machine? I'm in your city for two nights, and I wonder if you can give me a steer on restaurants?" Most people are happy to do it. Stay in touch with the people from your past. It's people who make life extraordinary. Not things.

Love,
Your Papa who's not lost in the past,
but who doesn't forget it

It takes effort to stay in touch.

Fads in the Stock Market

Alyssa and Wesley:

It isn't just stock markets that produce fads. We have them all through our lives: short skirts, long skirts, hula hoops, the Macarena, Nehru suits, oat bran, reality TV. Trading markets have produced fads since the beginnings of barter.

Some years ago, I had business in New York and went to have a nightcap in the Oak Bar at the Plaza Hotel. At midnight, every seat in the room was taken. Everyone there was drinking various amber-colored liquids, and virtually everyone, male and female, was smoking cigars. A year after that, I repeated the exercise, and almost no one was puffing on a cigar. The fad was now over.

Remember, no matter what you perceive as popular in society, be it certain sneakers, golf clubs, comic books, or personal computers, there are companies involved in those fads, and by buying their stock, you can profit while the fad lasts.

I have a client who owns an army-navy store in Chicago near one of the biggest and toughest projects on the South Side. He has made a small fortune understanding fads because, as he has told me, "All fashion among teens in America starts in the minority neighborhoods. What these kids are wearing, frankly, is where all the money is going to flow in the shopping malls frequented by the white, suburban, want-to-be copycats who think it's cool to dress like the boys and girls in the 'hood." Over the last ten years, he has been in and out of the stocks of Nike, Ralph Lauren, Target, Timberland, and Urban Outfitters, among others, getting in early and out as the fickle tastes of the kids changed.

Anything can become a fad in fashion or on Wall Street—just as women were induced to go for poodle skirts and bobby sox en masse in the 1950s, bobbed hair in the 1920s, miniskirts or hot pants in the 1960s. Wall Street over the years has gone into frenzies over bowling, double-knit fabrics, cable TV, conglomerates, franchising, railroads, antipollution, energy, and aerospace. You name it, and the group has had its day in the sun.

In the early 2000s, the biggest fad was the stock market itself, specifically the Standard & Poor's 500 index, made up of the biggest industrial companies. It had become a go-to benchmark, and few people bothered to study a little history about this fad. Recently, one of my best clients dropped by the office, accompanied by a so-called financial planner, a member of a profession that, in my opinion, is mostly long on charts and short on experience. The planner brought material loaded with bells and whistles and graphs showing that the client should have all of his equity money in an index fund that just tracked the popular averages.

"It's foolproof," the planner said. "Low cost and out-performs anything. Beat the Street the last two years, and you don't have to think about it."

"What did the stock market do in 1968?" I asked the planner.

He shrugged.

"What did the market do in 1982?" I asked.

"What difference does it make?" the planner said.

"Well," I said, "if you'd invested in an index fund, assuming such a thing existed in 1968, you still wouldn't have broken even *fourteen* years later. The Dow Indus-trials were one thousand in 1968 and nine hundred in 1982. Would you be prepared to lose money for your cli-ent for fourteen years?"

Fads seldom last more than two years, whether it's the S&P 500 or the Slinky. If the fad moves into a third year, it is really long in the tooth, and you'd better be prepared to take some profits and look for the next hot area. Does anyone even remember Davy Crockett? Or

Cabbage Patch dolls? These days, bonds seem a fad in themselves. Clients who'd never heard of a bond have been clamoring for them for a year and a half. They seem to be havens of safety in a volatile and scary world. Stocks are shunned, bonds are the rage. If you buy a so-called hot group two years into its popularity, the fad is usually closer to the end than the beginning. You can recognize a fad when everyone seems to be talking about it. Then plan your exit.

Your Papa, who's always searching
for the next fad

Fads last about two years.

Wesley Redux

Dear Grandson:

This Bud's for you, Wesley, and that's eventually okay, I suppose, because you're just a few years away from legal drinking age. Only two letters in this year of Papa as correspondent have not been addressed to both of you. I don't know if men are from Mars and women are from Venus, but I know there are incredible differences between the sexes.

Here's an observation that perhaps will not be popular with the politically correct crowd. But I do believe that certain things have been bred into us for thousands of years. In stock markets, we have had a decade of nonperformance, of averages that have basically flatlined. The last three years have been dominated by anxiety, which has led to fear and then to panic in the spring of 2009 on the part of investors.

During this panic period, when thousands of well-known, major companies sold for single-digit prices, I had a small number of clients who demanded to be sold out completely from stocks, literally within days of the absolute bottom. Almost every client who acted at the panic lows was a woman. My view of this is not that they were or are more emotional. They want to protect.

Women are bedrock. Their secret smiles I've seen over the years reveal that they understand so much more about what matters than we men. A woman friend who has been a CEO of retail companies told me once, "It's about childbirth that gives us the secret smile. Or even the thought of childbirth. That's the nature of nurturing, deep within us." The toughest career women I've known, who never thought they'd have children and were even cynical about it, suddenly did have children. Invariably they all said, "So *this* is what it's *really* all about."

Wesley, never take this enduring quality of women for granted. It is very powerful and will help you to understand them better.

I used to tell your father when he would pull stupid stunts in high school and college, like skateboarding in an empty swimming pool where he broke his wrist, "You've got a dumb gene somewhere. Every time you're about to do something dangerous or questionable, stop and say to yourself, 'Is the dumb gene about to kick in?'" He'd laugh with me, and the dumb gene has become a family joke. But he also agrees about the function of man as brontosaurus killer. I throw in this ramble as a caution about how to treat the women you love and will love in your life. In a love relationship, *never* say anything in haste or anger that will stick forever in the memory of this loved one. These are genies that you cannot put back in the bottle, and your dangerous words will be thrown back to you during almost every argument.

I've mentioned before, in terms of marriage, that a sense of humor is the most important quality in having a long-term relationship. Our friend Deedee Forbes (years ago, cute nicknames were all the rage) told me recently, "I've been married for fifty years, and we've survived because we learned to laugh together and to cry together. And after fifty years of marriage, to have separate bathrooms." You don't need to know this last bit for a long time. Right now you think that you're immortal. I'd never rain on that parade.

Many of your contemporaries I see or hear from seem much more interested in just "a job" than in pursuing a career that can take them up the ladder to what I call the "F" word. Every person who comes to see me as a potential client wants this one thing—*freedom.*

And so very few have it. Of course, they mean financial freedom.

You can achieve it several ways: inheriting it, making extraordinary investment wins, like Warren Buffett, hitting the lottery, or through incredibly hard work as an entrepreneur or businessman. For the average smart person, the first three ways are pipe dreams. Only the last will be really satisfying to you.

It wasn't me who wrote that "you're never really a man until you lose your father." But I can attest to the truth of this. The saddest day in my life to that point, when my father died suddenly, was also the most liberating day. I was now the father, no one between me and my fate. I was determined to leave something behind me that might survive my passing, and my passion for writing was fueled by this desire.

I met a man years ago in the locker room at the club where I played squash. He was Dr. John Knowles, and he had been head of the world-famous Massachusetts General Hospital. Later he became president of the Rockefeller Foundation in New York, one of the largest philanthropic organizations in America. John Knowles attacked life, in his profession and in his hobbies: golf, all racquet sports, playing the piano. He was the actor Jack Lemmon's roommate at Harvard. Here are a few of the things he taught me, and, since he was a doctor, CEO, and sportsman, I'm passing his wisdom on to you.

He had several mottos. One, quoted at his memorial service, was, "A sense of humor is a prelude to faith, and laughter is the beginning of prayer."

"I'll give you a scenario of life," he also told me. "You start off knowing that everybody is different, some pretty, some ugly, some smart, some dumb. Don't kid yourself about the prerogatives of power. I have to go halfway around the globe to meet Robert McNamara of the World Bank, then figure out how to feed millions of starving people. And the plane I'm supposed to go on is full. You better believe I'm gonna bump someone off that plane. You better believe they better find someone I'm more important than. If you're smart, then you go for the best. You go for the top. But you help people less fortunate all the way along, because that is the key to a successful life. Four elements: hard work, energy, use of the intellect, and humor. Jesus, if you can't laugh at yourself and the other poor bastards, you might as well dry up and blow away."

He appeared boyish. It was because of his energy, his restlessness, and the feeling that he was always ready to laugh, to see the ridiculous side of life. He knew life too well not to appreciate Jonathan Swift, the author of *Gulliver's Travels*. His view of the world was realistic, ironic. "You have to gather information from many

sources," he told me. "And you must never limit yourself to narrow vistas. I read constantly. Norman Mailer's
The Prisoner of Sex, Barzun's *House of Intellect*, every
week the *New York Times Book Review* to find out what
is being produced that makes us *think*. And I'll tell you
something about information. You better be a goddamn
good listener. People love to talk. I listen to cab drivers, doormen. The man in the street wants the American
dream. He doesn't want it handed to him on a government platter. Make your work your play. Enjoy it until
you don't anymore, then never be afraid of change.
Exercise. Blow the cobwebs out of your mind. If you
accumulate money, if you arrive economically, the hell
with it: go first class all the way. Don't feel guilty; you've
earned it."

John Knowles exuded confidence and good sense.
He had been controversial in his career, essentially
because institutions of any sort cannot stand too much
honesty. "Over ninety percent of us," he wrote once,
"are born healthy and made sick as a result of personal
misbehavior and environmental conditions." He went
on to say, "Most individuals do not worry about their
health until they lose it. Uncertain attempts at healthy
living may be thwarted by the temptations of a cul-
ture whose economy depends upon high production
and high consumption." Dr. Knowles quoted a study of
almost seven thousand adults over a five and a half year

period, relating health and longevity to the following regime:

1. Three meals a day at regular times and no snacking
2. Breakfast every day
3. Moderate exercise two or three times a week
4. Adequate sleep (seven or eight hours a night)
5. No smoking
6. Maintaining moderate weight
7. No alcohol or only in moderation

The day I saw him in his office, John Knowles looked down on the Avenue of the Americas. "Christ," he said, "life is to be enjoyed. Laughter, sex. God, the odor of sex overlays everything. But sex shouldn't be anxiety laden. It isn't quantity that counts. But have some discipline in your life. Have yearly checkups. Don't abuse your body with pills, drugs, tobacco." He laughed about style and talked about change and taking chances in life. "You have to step up to the plate," Dr. John Knowles said to me. "You have to do something with your life. Never forget," he added, "faint heart never slept with the cook. Think about this."

I have no problems in life, Wesley, with picking the best brains and the thoughts of smart men and women. And I write them down in small pocket notebooks. Not computers; dated notebooks with ideas, quotes, book recommendations, stocks, character studies. Not one bible. But dozens of little signposts I can look back on and continue to learn from.

Love,
Your Papa, who hopes you'll look back
on these letters and learn as well

Faint heart never slept with the cook.

Gold and Commodities

Dear Grandchildren:

There's no reason to think that either of you have ever thought about commodities. But you may have had a passing thought about gold, since the metal has been so much in the news for the past few years. My dad believed that everyone should own gold. He was frugal and tough, too, as I've told you many times. (It takes forever, you will find, to get over our childhoods.)

Dad didn't believe in debt; he didn't believe in life insurance, thinking it a horrible investment. But gold then, at $35 an ounce, he thought was a bargain. And, although frugal (he wouldn't buy shaving cream, just soaped his face with a shaving brush), he would buy your great-grandmother gold jewelry, bracelets, pins, necklaces, rings, always 24 karat to get the extra weight.

He bought gold cufflinks for himself, big and ornate, which I have now but do not wear. And one pair, small and intricate and lovely, sheaves of golden wheat, which I wear all the time. His rationale was that sooner or later, all governments debase their currencies, meaning that they print money willy-nilly, eventually causing inflation, through unwillingness to ever say "stop the madness" or say no to excess government spending. He was right. Gold now is worth about $1,800 an ounce. But it took years and years to get its price moving, long after my dad died. So, unless you invent something like Facebook, be prepared to be very patient on the road to riches.

But I began this letter talking of commodities. This category for investing includes iron ore, copper, aluminum, oil, and gas. Cattle, hides, pork bellies, orange juice, cotton. On and on the parade goes. And the swing in these prices can be extremely volatile, much more so than stocks. If either of you gets excited about any commodity and wishes to buy or sell any of them, including currencies of all sorts, I want you to take away one life lesson about this subject:

I have *never* in fifty years in the investment business ever seen an amateur trader of commodities do anything else but lose all of their money.

This may seem simplistic. But I do not think that either of you will be tempted to be a professional in the commodities business. Both of you probably *will* invest in stocks and bonds as the years pass. You may both even go into the financial world as bankers, even though I hope you don't. If you remain amateur investors through your adult lives, there are endless opportunities in a variety of places. If you must participate in commodities investing, here are a few gentler ways.

You can buy a managed futures fund. This means you can have outside, so-called experts run the money that you allocate to commodities. What does "futures" mean? You are betting on the future prices of corn, or sugar, or crude oil. All commodity investing is betting on the future, the same as betting on stocks, hoping the commodities rise in price. You can also bet on prices going down.

You can also buy an exchange-traded fund, an ETF, in almost any commodity you can imagine. For the average smart person, this is the sensible and relatively cheap way to go.

I have watched people blow themselves up in commodities for fifty years. Let's keep it simple. Never go out on a roof to fix it yourself, whatever it is. And never trade individual commodities to make a score.

So jump into commodity trading at your peril. Or try

it. It will make you think of your long-gone (probably) Papa and say to yourselves, "Papa was right."

Your commodity-wary Grandfather

I'd rather go to Vegas than trade commodities. At least in Vegas you can see a show.

Dealmaking: What's That All About?

Alyssa and Wesley:

So you want to make a deal, or you are curious about investment banking, or so-called private equity. Deal making can even include things in your lives like buying a condo or a house. What are some practical, down and dirty rules for this?

Here's one unconventional story about a friend of mine, Joe O'Donnell, who lives to keep people off balance when doing deals. Joe grew up in a blue-collar town, a tough town that believed in hard work, sports, and family. Joe is a billionaire and a former dean of students at Harvard Business School. Someone told me, in a kidding way, that Joe owns 4 percent of every deal in this city, from racetracks to restaurants, hotels to advertising agencies, from movies theatres to Dunkin' Donuts franchises. He has also endowed the baseball program at Harvard College, where, as an undergraduate, he captained the baseball team. He was, early in his career, a dean of students at Harvard Business School. His approach to business is eclectic and unique, like this story and his insistence upon making every transaction personal.

Joe and his wife were house hunting some years ago and they found what they wanted: a big Dutch Colonial with an acre of land. It had a swimming pool and a tennis court. "We wanted the house," Joe told me, "but you can't wear your heart on your sleeve. We saw it several times with the broker. And we made an offer. The owner countered, we made another offer, and we were still twenty-five grand apart. So I told the broker I wanted to eyeball the owner; look him in the face."

"We don't do that," the broker said.

"Fine," said Joe. "Good-bye to the house."

Joe told me, "It took the guy forty-five seconds and he was on the phone to the owner, settin' it up, even though he hated that the buyer would actually meet the seller in person. Not good for the deal, they think. So we meet at the house, Kathy and me, the broker, the owner, lookin' handsome and fit, and his wife, a babe."

"Well," the owner says, "it's nice to meet you both. But how does this change the deal?"

"You've got a tennis court," Joe says. "Do you play?"

"I do," said the owner.

"Tell you what," said Joe, "I've never seen you play. Look at me, out-of-shape, overweight. I got my brown lace-up shoes on. We're twenty-five thousand apart. Let's go out to your court; I'll play you two out of three games for twenty-five grand." Well, according to Joe, the owner looked like he was gonna pee his pants.

Joe went on, "The guy blinked. He wouldn't do it, wouldn't budge the price. I walked away. Most of the time in life they come back to you. This one didn't. And there's always another house. But the point is to always be a surprise. They'll *remember* you. And someone's always going to blink."

My client Billy Boyd has been an entrepreneur and deal maker all of his adult life. He was one of the founders of a large venture capital firm outside of Boston and was known, earlier in his career, for convincing an old Boston family to invest $9 million into an early cellular phone company. The $9 million eventually turned into a more than $2 billion bonanza for the family and their business. Here, grandchildren, are some of Billy's key principles of deal making:

1. *Scared money never wins; it's always afraid it's going to be taken away.* Think about this one: My father, for example, never got over the Great Depression. He beat it into me growing up that you had to save for a rainy day, that you mustn't

owe any money, that life was going to hammer you when you least expected it. He found it difficult to live and enjoy life because he was constantly looking over his shoulder for the next depression.

He repeated these themes so constantly that I was determined, when I grew up, to spend, travel, and live. And if it were all taken away from me, at least I would have attacked life in some small ways and be able to say, "Yup, I did that. I saw that. Before they took it all away from me."

Looking back at all this, I am surprised at the attitudes of that generation who were so colored by the Depression. During this period, my dad was in his early twenties, a time in people's lives where, if things go wrong, there is endless time, a long life ahead to come back, or thrive, or change things. If bad things happen to you in your twenties or thirties, and if you're willing to work hard and be positive, you will succeed; you can turn it around. If you want a model of how to lead an extraordinary life, read William Manchester's introduction to his book about Winston Churchill, *The Last Lion*. He recounts a day in Churchill's life at Chartwell, his country estate, prior to World War II when his countrymen had written him off as finished, an aging fool who didn't count anymore. This was before he became prime minister and emerged, in many minds, as the most important person of the twentieth century.

2. *In every deal, there's a pink Cadillac, and you'd better find out early on what it is.*

"Years ago, I was buying a radio station in Louisiana," Billy told me. "The seller was getting nervous."

"What's wrong?" Billy asked him.

"Well," he admitted, "my wife is upset at me." He was sheepish, and somehow I felt the deal slipping away.

"Tell me about it."

"Well," the owner of the station said, "every year we buy her a new pink Cadillac..."

So Billy immediately wrote into the agreement that the wife would get a new pink Cadillac annually.

3. *You should always back people in venture deals, not products.* People who back products usually lose. In the venture business, it's people; in the LBO (leveraged buyout—look it up, kids!) business, it's bringing the right person in. The great investors understand human nature better than they understand anything else.

4. *People with something to hide also make the best investors.* Insecure people, so conscious of their own image, are great at judging people. You under-

stand what *you're* trying to hide, so you tend to detect it in others.

Several years ago, I owned a large position in a women's personal care products company. After I was deep into the stock, I participated in a small meeting with the then chairman of the board. The chairman seemed so uncomfortable during this session that I had the distinct impression that he, if asked, would not describe what their very personal products actually did. I guessed he would either sell the company or take it down the drain. He did the former, thank goodness. But I always thought he sold it much too cheaply, just so he wouldn't have to tell anyone what he did for a living. If this implies *I'm* insecure, and I spotted it big time in him, so be it.

5. *In assessing companies, get to know the receptionist.* I'll sometimes ask a receptionist, "What does this company do?" You'd be amazed how many times the receptionist has absolutely no idea. When this person does know, and tells me lucidly, I know the company communicates well. It is the little touches that give you a feel for whether you invest in it or not.

The first time your Papa tried Billy's dictum, I was waiting to see an agent at one of the largest and most famous of the Hollywood/New York talent agencies. "What does this company do?" I asked the young lady.

She looked at me as if I were nuts.

"Huh?" she said. "Who do you want to see? I'm almost on my break."

I never signed with that agency.

6. *I believe in small companies; the optimum board of directors size is five people.* I would choose only one person from the company; two financial people whose role would be a continuous process of raising funds; one industry expert for obvious outside expertise; and one throwaway person chosen to provide comfort for everyone else.

What you should both take away from this letter is to try to think a little unconventionally. Remember the odd jobs you both had with people from all over the economic spectrum. Oftentimes, if you pretend you grew up in a triple-decker with fire in your belly, it will serve you both well.

Your Papa, who appreciates roads less traveled

Scared money never wins.

Stand Up for Yourselves

Wesley and Alyssa:

You guys have been raised comfortably. You went to wonderful schools. You went to summer camps and intensive sports weeks that all cost money. You went on family vacations unheard of when I was growing up, when the households in America did not seem to be run for the children, but for the adults. "There goes Papa again," you'll probably say, "on one of his rants on the younger generations." But what I mean to say is that the world doesn't care where lucky families went on spring vacations; very few people will ever *really* care for you. And growing up being used to plenty can be dangerous to a happy adult life. You will both have to do it yourselves, and stand up to make yourselves noticed. Here's a story that taught me an important lesson early in my business life.

Years ago, my original stock brokerage firm went

broke. It was in the early 1970s, a time for rising volume on the New York Stock Exchange, volume that could not be handled efficiently in the days before computers came into general use. The situation got so bad on Wall Street that if you bought one hundred shares of Colgate stock, you might end up with having 300 shares of Pfizer shipped to you by accident. Or your monthly statement would show numerous items you had never owned, or omitted many that were indeed yours. Or you would be sent checks for proceeds of stocks you had never ordered sold. Dozens of the oldest brokerage names in finance shut their doors, their business absorbed by fewer and fewer survivors.

I knew I'd have to prove myself in the new arena.

When I was in grammar school, in the fourth grade, we had a bully in our class named Dickie. He terrorized the smaller boys until a new youngster entered our class. He was wearing short pants, and Dickie teased him about being "a girl." The new kid got up onto his tip-toes one day after that and punched Dickie in the nose, which immediately gushed blood. All the other kids saw this and began chanting "Dickie Bloody Nose."

"My nose never bleeds," he cried. And he never really bullied anyone again.

I thought of the Dickie story because in my office I was warned, "Management in New York looks down on us and doesn't think anything outside of Manhattan is worth anything. It's tough getting them to take us seriously." I thought that if we're going to be bullied, I'd take myself down there and stick in my oar. I met with the chairman of our board and gave him several reviews of a few of my books by New York critics, including a column in *New York* magazine about me and my writings. "Wow," the Chairman said. "And you don't even live in the city." He meant New York.

"How about that?" I said.

There is something I call the "New York mentality," which doesn't always credit people from other places with too much of the right stuff. But New Yorkers will look at you differently, particularly if you ever get the nod from their media. It's very important to establish yourself as something perhaps different when you deal with potential bullies. Perception can be everything.

Never assume that if you do your job well, you'll be taken care of. There was a great character actor in Hollywood, Rod Steiger. A reporter asked him after he'd been acting for forty years, "What's the secret to a long career?" Steiger replied, "Every Monday morning I get up, determined to get out there and let them know I'm still alive."

Stand up for yourselves.

Your Papa, who tries to stand up every day

Don't be shy about sticking your oar in.

Heroes and Heroines

Alyssa and Wesley:

I cannot finish this year of letters without mentioning heroes and heroines. People who have inspired me, nurtured me, and taught me so much about what I've tried to pass onto you about money, business, and life. Both of you have mentioned to me a few people who have influenced you in special ways. They have always been teachers or coaches, which I consider wonderful, because they typically don't preach from on high. They tend to be inspirational, yet practical as well. I've talked somewhat in these letters about heroes and heroines. But I thought I'd share a few stories about what I've taken away from several really famous people who brushed your Papa's life when he was at his most vulnerable.

The first story is about another Papa: Ernest Hemingway. When I say I was at my most vulnerable age, for most of us this age is now for you, about to burst into the adult world, full of dreams and perhaps misconceptions. All I wanted to do at that young age was to sit in the cafés of Paris with a notebook and a drink and become the Great American Novelist. In the summer of 1959, I went to Pamplona, Spain, running with the bulls and searching for my Lady Brett. Hemingway was also there, the first time he had returned since *The Sun Also Rises* was published. That novel is in the top three that influenced me early in life.

Hemingway was traveling from corrida to corrida that summer, tracking the competition between Spain's leading matadors: Dominguin, the veteran, and Ordóñez, the young challenger. They were engaged in a series of shootouts, mano a mano, pursuing ears and tails. I knew that if I could get close to Papa, even for a few minutes, I could coax out of him the secret to literary fame and fortune. Problem was, he was constantly surrounded by an entourage that a friend described as "various picadors, reporters, suck-ups, and Smith College English majors."

I tracked the great man for three days looking for an opening—three days of running the bulls, enduring what seemed like a year's pressing of grapes squeezed into my mouth, my eyes, my ears, my shoes, my shirt from hundreds of wineskins. I cruised the plazas in anticipation. I slept in the back seat of a Simca, a car as unreliable as a weather prediction. I slept little and I drank large and I sat in the sun and I wondered about the people who could afford beds at night.

Then one evening, at about 10:30, I spied Hemingway exiting a café and heading for dinner. He rolled when he walked, swaggering like a high school football player. He moved away from his entourage suddenly, gesturing for it to wait while he swaggered down a side street. I followed and came upon him urinating next to a fountain off the main plaza. I stepped up to Papa and unzipped.

"Mind if I whiz next to you?" I asked.

Hemingway looked at me. "Whiz is what women do," he said. "Men piss."

"I actually want to write," I told him, "not whiz."

He snorted at me. "Let me tell you something, kid," he said. "Don't talk about what you want to do, do it. Run with the bulls. Watch the horns, like a fighter—feint, punch, feint, punch. Have a good leak, kid. Men also call a piss a leak. But whatever you call it, it's easier to do than writing," he said before rolling away.

The next afternoon, the sun was so strong it made me feel as if I were on another planet. I was sitting with two friends outside the bullring. They were drunk. Everyone in Pamplona was drunk. But my friends were the only ones in Pamplona getting their sneakers shined by three different shoeshine boys. In three different colors. Hemingway walked by, surrounded by a crowd of college students, Spanish companions, and other keepers of the flame.

"There's the Whizzer," he called to me, making his hangers-on jealous.

"You have your tickets?" he added.

"In the sun," I said.

"Watch how they feint," he said. "Watch how they feint, Whizzer." His entourage swept him along into the corrida.

At the time of my Pamplona adventure, probably the most famous actress in the world was Katharine Hepburn. She had won the most Oscars of any actress. You know and I know that the one thing any woman must understand about men is that they are all little boys. Some more than others, of course, and some keep it hidden better than their buddies. But it's lingering there, like the pimple you know is going to be showing on your chin by tomorrow morning. Your Mimi has a great talent in this regard, to cut through the nonsense. A few weeks ago, I showed her a picture in a magazine. "Look at this woman," I said, pointing at a model in an advertisement.

"I'm sure she's in her fifties and she's got shoulder length hair. Look how great it looks."

My wife looked at the picture, then at me. "Grow up," she said, and walked away.

She gets it, and, of course, this drives me nuts from time to time. But there was a moment in my life when it was okay for boys to be boys, even though they were dressed like girls. My senior year in college I was one of the female leads in the Hasty Pudding show, an original musical spoof written, produced, and performed annually since 1868 by male students. Jack Lemmon had acted in the show. And Fred Gwynne of *The Munsters* fame. Alan Jay Lerner, composer for *My Fair Lady*, wrote a show, as did Erich Segal, author of the best-seller *Love Story*. Traditionally, in the Hasty Pudding performances, men played all the female roles and there was always a kick-line number, which would be brought back for at least two, sometimes three, encores. And for years there has been a tradition of choosing a Woman of the Year at the Pudding, usually a famous actress, to get publicity for the show and to have an excuse for a party in the middle of the day.

That year, the honoree was to be Katharine Hepburn, who would accept her award (a small cast-iron pudding pot) onstage surrounded by selected cast members, including me in costume as the Duchess of Wopping, complete with glamorous tiara set on top of golden curls. Katharine Hepburn viewed the proceedings with wry amusement, the only real woman there and the only woman, fake *or* real, in pants. After the photographs, she watched us sing a few numbers, including my big hit song, done with my "husband," the Duke of Wopping. It was "The Abdication Waltz," and when it was over the great Hepburn took me by the arm and said, "Young man, I strongly suggest, when you graduate, that you go to law school," which in more recent times would be, "Don't give up your day job."

Hoping for any show business goodies that I could tuck away, I asked her if she had any suggestions for us men playing female characters. "Of course," she answered. "Read the female roles in Shakespeare. Everything you want to know about character and the theater is in Shakespeare." The party then moved on, into the bar for cocktails and music provided by the three-piece band whose members also played for the show's performances. Miss Hepburn was surrounded by people at the party, all trying, like me, to impress her. The room was dark and oak paneled, filled with old leather sofas and chairs sitting on even older oriental rugs. A long curved bar dominated one wall, facing a large walk-in fireplace with an oak mantelpiece. All the walls were covered with framed show posters dating back to the late 1800s, bearing names like *The Big Fizz*, *Love Rides the Rails*, and *Bombastes Furioso*. Many of us in the musical had visions of show business careers after college, thinking that life, like the Hasty Pudding Club, would be all fun and games.

After a few drinks, the band blaring out *The Lady Is a Tramp* and other songs likely played at coming-out parties, I decided to climb on top of the small upright piano. This would really let Katharine Hepburn see me strut my stuff, so that she would clearly want to be my friend forever. The band struck up the kick-line number and two chorus members joined me on top of the small upright. The room was cheering up until one of my high kicks collided with a hip-check from the dancing neighbor and I was launched off the piano into the band and actually went through the bass drum with my head. As I came up for air, the drummer literally began beating me with his sticks, yelling, "My *best* drum, my *best* drum," until we could be separated. After things settled down, Katharine Hepburn, ready to leave the event, came over to me and smiled the star's smile. "I said Shakespeare's *heroines*," she counseled, "not Shakespeare's *fools*." She gently tapped me on the hand with her little Pudding pot and was gone.

So what did these adventures teach me, before I went off into the real job world? Two lessons will benefit you in your long careers to come: One is, be mindful of the absurdities in life and how often they will occur. Two: Never take yourselves too seriously. Almost

every time I think I'm really smart, I get my tail handed
to me.

Love,

Your story-telling Papa

**Everything you want to know about
character is in Shakespeare.**

What About the Internet?

Grandchildren:

We are in more revolutions today, it seems, than ever before in history. And they all seem related to the Internet, from social networking to the upheaval around the world in places like Egypt, Syria, the Sudan, and elsewhere. I know from talking to both of you and seeing young people constantly who want to write or come in to the investment business that history is not very well taught today in American schools.

A few years ago I walked around the several floors of my firm's office and asked thirty younger employees, "Who is, or was, Winston Churchill?" Churchill, the former prime minister of Great Britain during World War II was arguably the greatest man of the twentieth century. Less than one-third of the people I asked about Churchill, *fewer than ten people*, male and female, could identify him. And only three of these knew anything other than fuzzy details.

When I talk about the importance of history, I also want to mention the importance of family history, and how most families' children and grandchildren really long for stories of ancestors long gone. And they realize this longing *after* relatives who could tell them about their roots have died. Get these stories from me, from your other grandparents, aunts, and uncles. Ask them about hard times, about music and movies and radio, TV, and sports. Ask them about the politics of earlier days. Ask them how they handled the hard stuff, and what gave them joy. Ask them if there is anything that *never* seems to change.

As for the Internet: Before this revolution, as I mentioned, there came electricity, the movies, radio, television, the personal computer. Not that long ago, Ronald Reagan was president. Russia, at the time, was the Evil Empire; the iron curtain of communism split the Western world. The Berlin Wall separated East Germany from West. CNN produced a revolution, in my opinion, in this instance. The people in East Germany could access CNN, and they saw endless shots of American consumers. They didn't focus on freedom in action. They focused on Americans buying things, having goods and services. And they wanted what they saw. The Berlin wall came down. Revolution. Because of consumer goods.

Now you're saying, in your busy young lives, "Papa, cut to the chase."

Okay, I will, with one more little story to illustrate my point. I had a problem with my computer in the last few days, and I hired a geek to come in and fix it. The geek had a law degree, had majored in philosophy in college, his eyes and ears out on sticks for endless adventures in life. As he wandered through my computer issues, fingers tapping, we talked about the Internet, various sites, and social networks.

"How do you think I got you?" I asked him. He shrugged. "I found you through a recommendation from a great woman friend. She said you were both smart and interesting, too. All life is relationships (my favorite theme, as you know), and you came from someone I trust. Not from the Internet."

He thought about that and said, "You know, you're right. Social networks for me leave a lot to be desired. By the way, did I tell you that my dad is the best in town at installing home entertainment centers? He's really good."

I trust my personal network, grandchildren. It's never

too early to start building your own team. Trust the actual face, not the book.

Your slightly fuddy-duddy Papa,
but a papa with a plan

Lose yourself in real life, not the virtual one.

Do What You Say You're Going to Do

Alyssa and Wesley:

Something happened to me this week that I had to pass on to you before I forget it. It's an important point in a short letter. Nice to give you a break once in a while with some brevity. A client of mine asked me if I'd help open a few doors for his son on a business venture the son had cooked up. I said, "Sure," and hooked him up with the chair of a foundation in Los Angeles who might help the young man market his specialty sneakers to third-world countries, where the foundation was focused.

"For opening this door," the young man said, "I'm eternally grateful. I'm gonna send you some red sneak-

ers with black laces. You'll love 'em." The connection
with the foundation was made and I was happy to
do the young ambitious man a favor. In a weird way,
I also was really looking forward to the red sneakers.
After almost two months, nothing arrived. The young
man's dad called me about something else and instead
of ignoring my encounters with his son, I said to him,
"You know, I wouldn't mention this to you, but your
son should know something that will help him in the
future."

"Oh, what's that?" the dad asked.

"As you know, I had a chat with him and made an
introduction for his business plan."

"Yup," the dad said. "He was very grateful."

"Well," I said, "he didn't have to say anything but
'thanks,' which he did. But he also told me he was sending me something from his catalog. So generous of him
and not necessary. But he never sent it. Also fine with
me. But this would stick in someone's brain whom he
may need later on in his career—a potential customer,
or a potential employer. Little things like not following
through on promises can come back to haunt you in
the future. The damnedest people have long memories.
Never burn your bridges."

It took two days for the red sneakers to arrive, and
my wearing them around town has gotten him other

orders from friends who liked the style. Word of mouth, if it isn't forced, can be the best sales technique.

Always follow through on your promises.

Love,
Your Papa with a long memory

Don't forget what you tell people, because they'll remember.

Long-Term Behavior

Dear Grandchildren:

There was a behavioral study that started in the 1940s called the Grant Study. It was initiated at Harvard and it was formed to track the behavior of 268 graduates from the classes of 1939–1944. The major purpose of the study was to discover if secrets of longevity and the keys to happy, productive lives could be discovered, and to see if healthy aging could be predicted. One of the participants was President John F. Kennedy.

The best-selling author and psychiatrist George Vaillant tracked the Grant Study and wrote two books on the subject, including the classic *Adaptation to Life*, which I recommend to both of you. The Harvard men were studied until they were eighty. Here are the real high points of the findings; I agree wholeheartedly with what these secrets to the good and long life are:

1. You should be active, not passive, in all your endeavors. Teddy Roosevelt was our president. He said, "Far better it is to dare mighty things, to win glorious triumphs, even though checkered by failure, than to take rank with those poor spirits who neither enjoy much or suffer much, because they live in the gray twilight that knows not victory nor defeat."

2. Love is extremely important. It need not be just married love, but love in as many of its forms as you can find.

3. You should be generous of spirit and generous with your wealth, if you attain it. The men studied who lived the longest were good at giving it away.

4. Stay involved in things; do not retreat into yourselves.

5. Take real vacations. Get away from what you do and from the people you see regularly. You need to "fill the cup" with travel, even if it's only short distances.

Dr. Vaillant described one of the study subjects, a man from San Francisco, who was gay and addicted to cigarettes and alcohol. But he described his long life by smiling and saying, "I sucked the lemon dry." What great words to live by.

Your Papa, trying to practice what he preaches

Suck that lemon dry.

Last Snippets to Ponder Before I Forget

Wesley and Alyssa:

Just a few last tales I'm pulling out of my story bag for you. I admit I'm envious of your youth and all the adventures you have in store. When I came out of college, it seemed that everything I had dreamed about was possible. I knew, or hoped, that hard work, desire, and some luck would pay off. I can honestly say that, looking back over my life, there is almost nothing important that I would have changed. Part of this was being lucky. So many choices I made, or were made for me, turned out to be the right ones. You never know.

One of these lucky moves was being in the business world for so long. This has enriched my life in so many unexpected ways, aside from building a net worth. It has been the accumulated wisdom of experiences that I never would have had if I had only been a writer.

If either of you are ever in the business world you will have clients. You'll find that your clients are the life-blood of your enterprise and must be constantly nurtured, because they are like children. When my parent company was American Express years ago, they hired McKinsey & Company for millions of dollars to find out what the clients really wanted. The answer was, "We want the company and our brokers to *pay attention* to us." Not "make us money," but "pay attention to us."

I've been working for fifty years and I still make house calls. Markets fluctuate, even though you two may want to own a little Apple and Google stock and scoff at your Papa for not listening enough to you. Guilty, of course. But this is about service to the clients, not picking stocks. And if, in your jobs, you are over the top with service and caring about them, you still can and *will* lose customers. It's inevitable. I've lost enough business over the years, I tell my partners, to have built up healthy emotional scar tissue that will last a lifetime. I can honestly say that in almost all cases, it was more about what was going on in people's lives than about investment performance. Not everyone will buy our advice, and many clients are not, no matter what they say, long-term oriented. So, know your characters, build up your own experience scar-tissue, and believe, as the character in *The Godfather* says, "It's not personal—it's business."

The second story I want to tell you involves one of

your Papa's true secrets about people. A client of mine years ago made a needlepoint pillow for me. The motto embroidered on it says, "You never know anyone until you deal with their money." It's true. Money brings out the best and the worst in people. Clients you thought would be tough turn out to be pussycats and your biggest supporters. Those who seem wonderful turn out to be disasters, with lives full of torment, which they often take out on you. In any business career it will be good to think about this perception of character. Another lesson in this: it may help you solve their problems in creative ways, and you get to hear amazing stories about how people live their lives.

Finally, a tale about the last shower. It was told to me by a successful entrepreneur friend whose many business triumphs have a lot to do with understanding human nature, and understanding his own nature as well. My friend played football at Harvard; he was an aggressive, tough lineman, raised by his parents to keep charging ahead, no matter what obstacles were put in front of him. He told me:

We were playing Princeton, knowing that if we beat them we would surely beat Yale and win the Ivy League Championship. The game was in their home stadium, and the day was rotten, cold with driving rain, the turf a sodden mud pit, like the trenches of World War I. At the end of the fourth quarter, we were deep in Princeton territory. I was exhausted, completely covered in mud, and practically blind from the winds and the wet. Then it was over. We lost. I walked back to the field house in tears of frustration and a certain anger. Then I realized I was about to take my last shower in an enemy locker room, my last chance for a victory on the road. I had desperately wanted a win for my senior year. And then, the hot water pouring over me: the last shower. And I thought, There will be many last showers in my life in front of me. And I should savor them all as certain bench marks to remember, win or lose.

Alyssa and Wes, you'll have many last showers as well, in defeat and victory. Cherish the memories.

I love you both and will take joy in all you give to and take out of your adventures.

Papa

You never know anyone until you deal with their money.

About the Author

JOHN D. SPOONER is probably the best-known investment advisor/writer in America. His bestselling books include *Confessions of a Stockbroker*, *Smart People*, and *Sex and Money*, and the novels *Class* and *The Foursome*. His articles have appeared regularly in magazines such as *Playboy*, *Town and Country*, *The Atlantic Monthly*, *Esquire*, *Time*, and *The Boston Globe*. He has been a director of *The Atlantic Monthly* and David Godine Publishers and a member of the Massachusetts Cultural Council, which distributes all arts funding for the Commonwealth. He has been honored with the Literary Lights Award, given to New England's most distinguished writers by the Boston Public Library.

A managing director of a major Wall Street firm, Mr. Spooner was the creator of *A Book for Boston*—a celebration of Boston's 350th birthday. He lectures widely and has appeared on numerous TV and radio programs, including *Wall Street Week*, Fox News, and NPR. Currently, he serves as a guest commentator on Bloomberg National Radio. Spooner was on the board of the Harvard Alumni Association and was a co-founder of The Curious George Foundation.

Spooner has been a contributing editor for *Worth* magazine and the business editor of *Boston* magazine. His book *Do You Want to Make Money or Would You Rather Fool Around?* was a *Boston Globe* bestseller and translated into foreign editions in Hungary, China, Japan, and Portugal. The *Improper Bostonian* magazine voted Spooner Boston's Best Investment Advisor. *Barron's* named him one of the 100 Best Investment Advisors in America.

Mr. Spooner watches over portfolios for more than two thousand people all over the world. A graduate of Harvard, he lives on Beacon Hill in Boston.

**BUSINESS
PLUS**

Recognized as one of the world's most prestigious business imprints, Business Plus specializes in publishing books that are on the cutting edge. Like you, to be successful we always strive to be ahead of the curve.

Business Plus titles encompass a wide range of books and interests—including important business management works, state-of-the-art personal financial advice, noteworthy narrative accounts, the latest in sales and marketing advice, individualized career guidance, and autobiographies of the key business leaders of our time.

Our philosophy is that business is truly global in every way, and that today's business reader is looking for books that are both entertaining and educational. To find out more about what we're publishing, please check out the Business Plus blog at:

www.bizplusbooks.com